AN

ESSAY ON EQUITY

IN

PENNSYLVANIA.

BY ANTHONY LAUSSAT, JR.
STUDENT OF LAW, MEMBER OF THE LAW ACADEMY OF PHILADELPHIA.

Quærens omnia, dubitans plerumque, et mihi diffidens.
Cic. Acad. Quæst. 1.

THE LAWBOOK EXCHANGE, LTD.,
Union, New Jersey
2002

ISBN 1-58477-139-9

Printed in the United States of America
on acid-free paper

The Lawbook Exchange, Ltd.
965 Jefferson Avenue
Union, New Jersey 07083-8605

Please see catalogue at rear of this volume
or our website
www.lawbookexchange.com
for a selection of our other fine facsimile reprints
of classic works of legal history.

Library of Congress Cataloging-in-Publication Data

Laussat, Antony, 1806-1833.
An essay on equity in Pennsylvania / by Anthony Laussat, Jr.
p. cm.
Originally published: Philadelphia: Robert Desilver, 1826.
Includes bibliographical references.
ISBN 1-58477-139-9 (cloth: alk. paper)
1. Equity—Pennsylvania. I. Title.

KFP85 .L3 2001
346.748'004—dc21 00-067115

AN
ESSAY ON EQUITY
IN
PENNSYLVANIA.

BY ANTHONY LAUSSAT, JR.
STUDENT OF LAW, MEMBER OF THE LAW ACADEMY OF PHILADELPHIA.

Quærens omnia, dubitans plerumque, et mihi diffidens.
Cic. Acad. Quæst. 1.

PHILADELPHIA:
PUBLISHED FOR THE INSTITUTION,
BY ROBERT DESILVER.
R. WRIGHT, PRINTER.

1826.

TO

The Honourable WILLIAM TILGHMAN, LL. D. Patron,

PETER S. DU PONCEAU, LL. D. Provost,

JOSEPH HOPKINSON, LL. D.
AND
BLOOMFIELD M'ILVAINE, Esq. } Vice Provosts,

OF THE LAW ACADEMY OF PHILADELPHIA,

THIS ESSAY

IS RESPECTFULLY DEDICATED.

PREFACE.

The following essay has no higher pretensions than those of an academical exercise. It was a duty *imposed* upon the writer by his superiors, as an introduction, it is presumed, to a more extended view of the science of the law than is usually obtained by a course of elementary reading. It is hoped that this circumstance will sufficiently apologize for the bold ground that has been taken, which in any other situation, might justly have been deemed unwarrantable presumption.

As the publication of this Essay is also to be ascribed, exclusively, to those who are at the head of our institution, the writer trusts that he will be acquitted from the imputation of a desire to obtrude himself upon an enlightened profession, from whom he has yet much to learn, and whom he certainly will not presume to instruct.

It may, perhaps, be thought, that the distribution of this Essay should have been confined to the members of the law Academy and their friends, as is usual in similar cases: to this objection, the writer can only answer, that it is published by the institution, and not by himself; and that they had, no doubt, sufficient motives for the course they have thought proper to adopt.

The difficulties presented by the subject of this Essay, must be well known to every member of the Bar of Pennsylvania; and when united to inexperience, will serve as some apology for the many failures of the writer. For whatever could have been achieved by mere industry exercised during many months, he requests no favour; but the profound knowledge, which is the result of long study and deep meditation, can neither be expected nor found in the following pages.

If the writer be so far successful, as to draw to this important subject, the attention of those who are more capable of its investigation, he will rejoice that he has been thus able to discharge in advance the heavy debt, which, according to Sir Edward Coke, every lawyer owes to his profession and his country.

Philadelphia, April 11th, 1826.

LAW ACADEMY OF PHILADELPHIA.

The Provost and Vice Provost appoint, as the subject of dissertations to be prepared during the ensuing recess. EQUITY IN PENNSYLVANIA, under which head the nature and extent of the Chancery powers of our state judiciary, and the manner in which they are exercised, are to be considered. The subject is to be treated in an historical as well as legal point of view, and the whole reduced to a system, under proper divisions. The question whether in Pennsylvania a separate court of chancery is indispensably necessary, is to be considered; and in case the writer maintains the negative, he is to point out the manner in which it may be supplied.

PETER S. DU PONCEAU.
THOMAS SERGEANT.

Philadelphia, April 6th, 1825.

The Provost and Vice Provost have read with great attention the Dissertation on Equity in Pensylvania, which has been sent to them by one of the members of the Law Academy. They regret that although eight gentlemen were appointed to prepare similar dissertations, no other has been produced, and therefore there can be no question of comparative merits.

In justice to the Academy, however, they must say, that this Dissertation, the author of which is unknown to them, does great credit to his talents. It exhibits much research and investigation. a good method and a correct style; and the observations that it contains are in general sensible and judicious.

The Provost and Vice Provost are of opinion that it would tend to produce emulation among the members of the Academy, and give a favourable idea of our institution abroad, if this Essay were published under its direction.

PETER S. DU PONCEAU.
THOMAS SERGEANT.

Philadelphia, Oct. 13th, 1825.

AN

ESSAY ON EQUITY

IN PENNSYLVANIA.

Equity, in its most comprehensive acceptation, includes the whole circle of moral and civil obligations, and is the end, to the attainment of which, all laws should be directed. The moral law, founded upon the immutable principles of natural justice, owes its origin to equity; while municipal regulations depend upon it for construction, and are directed through its medium to the objects upon which they are to act. Considered in this extensive sense, equity is synonymous with justice, and to distinguish it from law, the means of its attainment, would convey a mistaken opinion of the moral rectitude of our jurisprudence. A new and technical signification, implying a power of a peculiar nature, has been affixed to the word; the origin, necessity, and universality of which, can be shown by a brief historical deduction.

B

The first necessity of men, at their original connexion by the bond of civil society, was a system of laws suited to the nature of their pursuits, in order to protect the simple from the artifices of the crafty, and the weak from the aggressions of the strong. Mutual intercourse, intermarriages, and commerce, naturally drew together these patriarchal communities; and when an union of many had constituted a nation, the increase of subjects for the operation of laws, and the progress of civilization, caused an extension of their simple regulations; while the experience they possessed dictated the means of their enforcement.

But though the result of the wisdom of ages, human laws, partaking of the common frailty of the institutions of men, must naturally be defective. Every rule of action must have a definite end, beyond which it cannot without injury be extended; while the objects upon which it is to act, in their circumstances and parts, are infinitely various, New cases must therefore sometimes occur, unforeseen by the written law;* and others, wherein a strict adherence to the general rule would create a particular injury, and make the *summum jus*, according to the old legal maxim, *summam injuriam*.† A new power is therefore necessary to remedy the defect, and

* Neque leges, neque senatus consulta ita scribi possunt, ut omnes casus qui, quando que inciderint, comprehendantur.—1 10 ff de legibus.

† Habeant similiter curiæ prætoriæ, potestatem tam subveniendi contra rigorem legis, quam supplendi defectum legis. Si enim porrigi debet remedium, ei quem lex preætriit, multo magis ei quem vulneravit.—Bacon de Aug. Scient. L. 8, c. 3. Aphorism 35.

by a recurrence to natural principles for a sound interpretation of the law, to prevent its unintentional harshness, when applied to a particular case; this is the power to which we affix the name of equity. It is not a superior power, rising in sullen majesty above municipal regulations, without impediment or restraint, but merely a subservient principle not called into action, until by reason of its universality, its superior is deficient.*

The power of dispensation, to which that branch of equity which mitigates the severity of law, would at first view appear to bear some resemblance, is, in truth, very dissimilar. Dispensation annuls the obligation of the law, equity points out the exceptions in which the obligation does not hold; the one counteracts the will of the legislator, the other, by a sound interpretation of his intention, averts it from an improper action upon unexpected cases. Dispensation by its mere power exempts a person or thing from the action of the rule; equity, like the Roman prætor, is "custos, non conditor legis; juvare, supplere, interpretari, mitigare jus civile potuit, mutare vel tollere non potuit."†

When, therefore, the subject of complaint is the *necessary* and *immediate* result of a law founded upon ge-

* Grotius defines equity to be "correctrix ejus, in quo, lex propter universalitatem deficit; fit autem ea correctio, non tollendo legis obligationem, sed declarando legem, in certo casu, non obligare."—De Æquitate, Sec. 12.

† For the distinction between Equity and Dispensation, see Grotius, de Indulgentiâ S. I. 4. and Puffend:—Elementa Jurisp. Univ. L. 1. S. 22. 23.—The quotation I have made from the civil laws is to be found Dig. I. 1. tit. 1. 7.

neral principles, equity cannot arrest its progress; but where the injury is *collateral*, so that it may fairly be presumed to have been unforeseen by the legislator, this beneficent power may interfere for the advancement of justice.*

If then a distinction be drawn between courts of law and equity, it is not to be presumed, that the one judges according to the strictness of the rule, without regard to natural justice, and the other according to equity, without regard to the rule; but we are to consider them as courts, the one of which has jurisdiction of the general law, while the other is confined to those instances, which either are or were strictly exceptions, and for which no proper provision had been made by the ordinary rules; these and these only, are within the power of equity; for they are the only cases which, in the words of Grotius, "lex non exactè definit, sed arbitrio boni viri permittit."

The rise of equity being therefore the natural consequence of the existence and imperfections of positive law, it follows that it must find a place in the judicial system of every well constituted government. It was known to the Greeks, and is mentioned by Aristotle in words of which the definition commonly ascribed to Grotius, is but a translation.† The Romans had their Jus Prætorium, a collection of rules introduced by the prætor, to supply and correct the municipal law for

* 2 Swift's System, 423.

† The words of Aristotle are Καὶ ἐςὶν αὕτη ἡ φύσις ἡ τȣ ἐπιεικȣς, ἐπανορθωμα νομȣ ᾗ ἐλλειπει διὰ τὸ καθολȣ.—Barb. Puffend. L. 5, c. 12. S. 21.

the public welfare.* In Scotland, the power of equity originally exercised by the king in council, is now vested in their supreme court, the court of session.† In France, the superior courts of justice which, before the revolution, were called parliaments, and are now denominated *Cours Royales*, administer law and equity at the same time, and under the same judicial forms: and in Portugal, the council of conscience reviewed the decisions of other courts, and moderated them by the principles of equity.

The Saxon and Danish monarchs of England, personally held courts of judicature, in which they decided both according to the ordinary law, and the justice and equity of the particular case.‡ As this double duty gradually became cumbersome, King Edgar restricted his jurisdiction to equity only, by directing that no appeal should be made to him when the party could obtain justice in the ordinary courts; but if the law dealt too hardly by him, he might then apply to the throne for its moderation.§

At the Norman conquest, the supreme judicial power both of law and equity, was vested in the Aula regia, and there continued, until the dissolution of that court, and the partition of its jurisdiction by King John, at the instance of his turbulent barons. The power of

* L. 7. § 1 de justitia et jure.

† Kames' Princ. of Equity, 23.

‡ Leges Canuti Regis. fol 108. Lambard's Saxon Laws, fol. 79. Bohun's Curs. Cancellariæ, 2.

§ Nemo ad regem appellet pro aliqua lite, nisi jus, domi consequi non possit. Si jus nimis severum sit, alleviatio deinde quæratur apud regem. 7th Law. Lamb. c. 2 fol. 79.

mitigating the law then returned to its ancient channel, the king,—assisted by the chancellor and council.* The ignorance and inefficiency of the monarchs, the invention of uses, the strictness of the common lawyers, and the ambition of the clerical chancellors, enabled the latter, about the reign of Edward III. to separate themselves from the council, and to erect a new and distinct jurisdiction.†

It was this separation that laid the foundation of the present system of equity, and caused the singular spectacle of two laws governing the same kingdom, varying with the jurisdiction to which the application for redress is made, and thus creating *imperium in imperio*. The court of chancery encouraged by its first successes, rapidly extended its usurpations, and soon changed the whole face of the judicial system. The original end of equity being to correct the defects arising out of the universality of the law, in its unsophisticated state, each case should be decided upon its own peculiar circumstances: and it was in this manner that the court of chancery proceeded, even in the time of Lord Bacon. To reduce it to positive rule, it was thought, would destroy its very essence, and render necessary a new court of conscience in order to administer equity in those special cases in which the principles of the first operated with unjust severity. This is certainly our idea of a judicial establishment in its perfection; and were judges more than men, it is thus that even the law should be administered. But

* Rex-*v*-Standish. 1 Lev. 242. 1 Harrison's Chancery, 7.

† Lambard's Archaion. 62.—Cases in Equity abridged, tit Courts. B.

unfortunately the weakness and fallibility of human nature make it impossible in practice. "The discretion of a judge," said Lord Camden, "is the law of tyrants; it is always unknown, it is different in different men; it is casual, and depends upon constitution, temper and passion. In the best it is oftentimes caprice, in the worst, it is every vice, folly and passion, to which human nature is liable."* A general rule when applied to a particular case, will sometimes cause an unjust judgment; but it is a less inconvenience, than that the decree should float, as it were, upon a sea of uncertainty, without pilot or rudder to protect it from the dangers to which the frailty of the bark exposes it. A court of equity, by introducing refinements upon the law, is certainly of considerable advantage; but the good of mankind requires that there should be some definite end to this power, and when that is attained, new courts cannot be infinitely instituted to form checks upon each other.† "Optima est lex," says Bacon, "quæ minimum relinquit arbitrio judicis optimus judex, qui minimum sibi."‡ If equity had continued to depend upon the arbitrary discretion of a single judge, and was measured by the breadth of his conscience, the experience of its

* Bacon expresses the same opinion. Maxime autem interest certitudinis legum, (de qua nunc agimus,) ne curiæ prætoriæ intumescant et exundent in tantum, ut prætuxtu rigoris legis mitigandi, etiam robur et nervos, iis incidant, aut laxent, omnia trahendo ad judicium.—De Aug. Scient. L. 8, c. 3. aph. 43.

† Lord Hale says, "by the growth of equity upon equity, the heart of the common law is eaten out."

‡ De Aug. Scient. L. 8 c. 3. Aph. 46.

disadvantages would long ago have procured its abolition.

The progress of equity in the prætorian courts of Rome, strongly illustrates the necessity of settled principles to govern this otherwise wild discretion. Each cause which required its interference, was originally decided upon its own basis; but corruption and partiality introduced abuses, and the tribune Cornelius caused a law to be enacted, obliging the prætors to adhere to the rules of judgment, which it was their custom to inscribe in an album, at the commencement of their respective offices.*

The court of chancery in its progress, soon felt the like necessities. Of the numerous cases over which it had begun to assume jurisdiction, many involved the same facts and circumstances; and certain rules in consequence gradually arose, to which succeeding judges submitted, either from a sense of their intrinsic wisdom, or a becoming diffidence of their own opinions. When these rules had caused transfers of property, it became necessary to adhere to them, in order to prevent uncer-

* Du Ponceau's Butler, Appx. Note 3, p. 133. Bacon approves highly of this alteration. Non sine causa, in usum venerat apud Romanos, album prætoris in quo præscripsit et publicavit, quomodo ipse jus dicturus esset. Quo exemplo, judices in curiis prætoriis, regulas sibi certas (quantum fieri potest) proponere, easque publice affingere.—De Aug. Sci. L. 8, c. 3, 46. In the code Napoleon, judges are forbidden to lay down general principles; "Il est defendu aux juges de prononcer par voie de disposition generale et reglementaire sarles causes, qui leur sot soumises."—Tit. Prelimin. Art. 5.

tainty, even, perhaps, though the original reason had been lost; and so far have this necessity and its consequence been pushed, that in cases of fraud and trust, which from their very nature, must be almost infinitely various, the courts constantly proceed upon a clear and distinct principle.*

This important revolution completes the second stage of equity, and its parent the court of chancery. The latter is no longer a court deciding each case upon its own peculiar foundation, and invested only with a jurisdiction of exceptions; while the former has attained the dignity of a science, based upon principle, and administered with liberality. The definition of equity, given by Aristotle, "a correction of the law, where by reason of its universality, it is deficient," no longer conveys an exact idea of its signification: it is a system of improvements upon the ordinary rules of law, introducing new maxims and powers, for the better administration of justice.

As this beneficial change was completely effected, before the settlement of Pennsylvania, when we examine, (as I now propose to do,) the subject of the introduction of equity by our predecessors, we must understand by it the stated principles which constitute the second and most refined species. The modes of proceeding of courts of equity, both in England and in the United States, are a subject of a different consideration, and not immediately connected with the design of this essay.

* Bond-*v*-Hopkins, 1 Sch. and L. 428. Heard-*v*-Stamford, 3 P. Wms. 411. Wagstaff-*v*-Wagstaff, 2 P. Wms. 258.

THE HISTORY OF EQUITY IN PENNSYLVANIA.

The Charter of Pennsylvania is a noble monument of the confidence of a British monarch, in the wisdom and probity of our founder and benefactor. The power of legislation, the highest act of sovereignty which one man can exercise over another, the appointment of judicial officers, the right of pardon and reprieve, the power of incorporating towns and creating ports, the receipt of customs, and the supreme military command, were vested in him almost without restriction; and the province became a principality, of which the proprietary was Palatine. But, as from the occupations incident to the settlement of a new country, the task of legislation could not be immediately commenced, the law of England relating to the regulation and government of property, the descent and enjoyment of lands, and the succession and possession of chattels, was declared to be the law of the province, until altered by the proprietary with the consent of a majority of the colonists, or their delegates.*

Equity, an unquestionable branch of the common law of England,† thus became a part of the law of Pennsylvania. The mode of administering it, and consequently the extent of its powers, was left as a matter of secondary importance, to the discretion of the proprietary.

The fifth section of the charter had vested in him

* Charter of Pennsylvania, Section 6.

† Pollard-*v*-Shafer, 1 Dall. 211, 213, 214. The United States-*v*-Coolidge 1 Gall. 489. Opinions of Provost of L. A. Book A, 114.

the right of appointing judges and establishing courts, with such powers and forms as should seem to him most convenient; and it is obvious from this clause, thus generally expressed, that a court of chancery might have been erected, had it accorded with the policy of Penn, or the principles which prevailed at the settlement of the province. But such was not the case. Our predecessors were men of plain, though useful information, and the nature of their prior avocations had not been such as to acquaint them with the formalities of a court of chancery, a perfect knowledge of which, is so necessary to its judge. In addition to this difficulty, the nature of such a court is averse to simplicity of proceeding, which was the great and wise object of the proprietary, in his judicial establishments.

The causes of the friends, who were a very large majority of the colonists at that early day, were usually decided by an appeal to the meeting of their persuasion, and the only process used to compel submission to an award, was the censure of the society, and a privation of privileges. Another mode, which was however established by law for the general use of the colonists of all persuasions, was by the decision of three officers, called peace-makers, appointed at each county court, whose duty was to hear and determine all controversies, in the manner of common arbitrators.*

The celebrated lord Peterborough, who, in order to conceal his intrigues for the dethronement of King

* Penn's Letter to the Free Society of Traders. 1 Proud's Hist. 262.

James, made a circuitous voyage to Holland, by the way of Pennsylvania,* gives a singular account of the condition of the province at that early period. "I took a trip once," says he, "with Penn, to his colony of Pennsylvania; the laws there are contained in a small volume, and are so extremely good, that there has been no alteration wanted in any one of them, ever since Sir William made them. They have no lawyers. Every one is to tell his own case, or some friend for him; they have four persons as judges on the bench, and after the case has been fully laid down on all sides, all the four are to draw lots and he on whom the lot falls decides the question. 'Tis a happy country, and the people are neither oppressed with poor's rates, tythes, nor taxes."† I must add, however, that this statement is supported by no other authority.

The year 1684 is marked by the establishment of a provincial court, which uniting in itself the jurisdiction both of law and equity, gave birth to our present mixed system.‡ By this union it was proposed to obtain the advantages of the latter, without its inconveniences. The proceedings, so far as they can be traced, were according to the ordinary legal forms, without the application to the consciences of the parties,§ and stripped of those numerous causes of delay which constitute at the present time, the most important barrier to the erection of a court of chancery. The commission of the

* Siécle de Louis XIV. Chap. 20.

† Spence's Anecdotes, 155.

‡ 1 Journal of Jurisprudence, 59.

§ Rawle's Address, p. 13.

five judges of the court, granted to them by the proprietary immediately before his return to England, limited the duration of their officers to two years, and the continuance of their good behaviour.*

But these simple and irregular establishments, could not long exist. Settlers increased, the country improved, and as a consequence of rising wealth, the spirit of litigiousness grew up.† The composition of the colony began to vary materially; and of necessity there were many upon whom as they differed in persuasion, the meetings could exercise no jurisdiction. The provincial court was found by experience to be extremely ill organised and inefficient. In 1685, as two of the judges refused to serve, and the third was prevented by sickness, the council were themselves obliged to hold the court at the stated time; and afterwards a custom arose which continued for several years, to commission judges for a single session.‡ The decision of controversies by stated arbitrators was attended with practical disadvantages; and it became necessary to resort to other and more effectual means.

* 1 Proud's History, 286-7.

† In a message of the 1st of January, 1723, Governor Keith complained to the assembly of the great increase of law suits, (2 Votes 335.) It appeared on examination, (2 Votes, 337) that from September 1715, to September 1716, the number of writs issued, had been 431, which, when the population of the colony is taken into consideration, was a very large number. In the year between September 1721, and September 1722, they had increased to 847; and from that time to December of the same year, 250 had issued.

‡ Minutes of council, 1 Journal Jurisprudence, 60.

A number of acts establishing courts of judicature, passed the provincial assembly at various periods; but their uniform repeal by Queen Anne, in council, increased the embarrassment of the judicial system.* Among others of these ephemeral courts, in the year 1715, a supreme court of law and equity was established,† which four years afterwards, shared the fate of its predecessors.‡

At the accession of Sir William Keith to the government of the province, the confusion of the judiciary had reached an alarming height, and was the cause of great injury and suffering to the colonists. No courts, with the single exception of the city quarter sessions, had been held for many terms back; and a prompt and vigorous exercise of the power with which the governor was invested, had grown to be a matter of the first necessity.§ Courts of law, both of inferior and superior jurisdiction, were immediately erected; and the lapse of a few months suggested to his mind, so fertile in expedients, an innovation upon the system, of which our predecessors had before entertained no idea.

It was in a message to the assembly of the province, bearing date in 1720, that he first suggested the propriety of erecting a court of chancery.‖ A resolution of the house having approved the proposition, and re-

* Index to Galloway's Laws, Tit "courts."

† 2 Votes of Assembly, 171.

‡ 1 Galloway's Laws, 74.

§ 3 Votes of Assembly, 270.

‖ 2 Ibidem, 270.

quested its establishment,* he issued his proclamation, creating the court, granting to it the same powers and jurisdiction as that of England, and appointing a day for its session.†

The constitution of this court was very peculiar, and affords a striking instance of the irregularity of judicial proceedings at that early period. All the members of the council in or near Philadelphia, were summoned to assist the governor, who, in imitation of the governors of other provinces, claimed the chancellorship as a matter of right;‡ and no decree could be made but by him, with the assent and concurrence of at least two of the six eldest of his assistants. These six were also to be employed as masters in chancery.§

Of the proceedings of this court, thus established at the general desire of the legislature of the province, but little has survived to us; that little, will however serve in part to explain the obloquy into which it subsequently fell, and the causes which moved to its final abolition.

In 1725, John Kinsey, an eminent lawyer of the society

* 2 Votes of Assembly, 71.

† Ibidem, 273.

‡ In 1705, Lord Cornbury, the governor of New Jersey, separated the court of chancery, from the court of common right, of which it had been a branch, and ordained that it should thereafter be held by the governor and council. The powers of chancery were also exercised by the governors of New York and South Carolina.—Smith's Hist. of New York, 253.—1 Ramsey's South Carolina, 95.

§ 3 Votes of Assembly, 255.

of friends, afterwards chief justice, was compelled by Sir William Keith, to take off his hat, before he would allow him to address the court, in a cause in which he was concerned. This appears to have caused great consternation in the province, since at their next quarterly meeting, the society appointed a committee to address the governor, and to require of him the free exercise of the privilege to which they were entitled by law, of appear-in courts or otherwise, in their own way, and according to their religious persuasion.* It was the policy of Sir William Keith to court the favour of the people, and in consequence, a rule of court ensured to the aggrieved, full liberty in this point of conscience.†

That the business of this court was never extensive, may be inferred from the circumstance that during the nine years Governor Gordon (Keith's successor) presided, but two suits (and those by consent) were brought to a decree: and the extraordinary chancery powers were rarely resorted to.‡ The people were however dissatisfied; the contests between the proprietary and colonists were then at their height, and every power exercised by the servants of the former was necessarily scrutinized with a jealous eye. On the 17th January, 1736, sixteen years after the establishment of the court, petitions from the counties of Philadelphia and Bucks, were presented to the assembly,§ complaining of the court of chancery, as a violation of the charter of privi-

* Sixth law agreed upon in England.—1 Votes of Assembly, 32.

† 2 Proud's Hist. 200.

‡ 3 Votes of assembly, 269.

§ Ibidem, 250.

leges granted to the people of the province. The county of Chester joined in the remonstrance,* and a resolution passed the house requiring from the governor, information as to the manner in which the court had been constituted. The sixth article of the charter was that referred to by the petitioners; it was there provided that no person or persons should or might at any time thereafter, be obliged to answer any complaint, matter or thing whatsoever relating to property, before *the governor and council,* or in any other place, but in the ordinary course of justice;† and it was contended, that the court of chancery was a direct violation of the article. On the 27th January, the house having received the requisite information, resolved, "that the court of chancery, as *then established,* was contrary to the charter of privileges."‡

A very elaborate and angry reply to this resolution, prepared by the council at the instance of the governor,§ was satisfactorily answered by a committee of the house;|| and with this, the contest appears silently to have terminated. Governor Gordon died shortly afterwards, and the decision and reasons of the assembly were submitted to by Mr. Logan, who, as president of the council, succeeded him. An act was passed confirming the changes of property, which had taken place in consequence of the decisions of the late court of chan-

* 3 Votes of Assembly, 253.
† 1 Galloway's Laws, 9.
‡ 3 Votes of Assembly, 258.
§ Ibidem, 269.
|| Ibidem, 273.

cery;* thus quieting the only objection which could have been raised to the mode of its abrogation.

In this manner was abolished the first, perhaps the last Pennsylvanian court of chancery, and it is easy to perceive from a slight view of the papers interchanged upon this subject, that the true, though hidden cause, was a jealousy of the governor entertained by the people. Appointed by the proprietary, and subject to removal at his pleasure, it was natural that he should favour the interest of him upon whom he depended; and the consequence was a loss of popular favour, and a suspicion of the integrity of his conduct. So long as the court remained under the direction of Sir William Keith, who had obtained the good opinion of the colonists by an attachment to their interests, no murmurs or complaints were heard; but the accession of a governor more favourable to the proprietary, was the signal for the bursting forth of a flame which had been concealed, not extinguished.

But though the court and proceedings of chancery were abolished, the principles of equity continued a part of the colonial jurisprudence, and we find the legislature very early desirous of preventing the confusion, which they supposed might ensue from an union of law and equity in one tribunal. It appears by the votes of the house of assembly, that on the 7th of February 1736, a bill for establishing a supreme and an inferior court of equity, passed its thiid reading.† The inferior court was to have been composed of the jus-

* 3 Votes of Assembly, 269.

† 3 Votes, 258 and 261.

tices of the respective county courts, who were to determine all matters in equity under the value of one hundred pounds. The supreme court was to have had appellate jurisdiction from the inferior, and to have taken cognisance originally of such suits in equity, in which the value of the thing demanded exceeded one hundred pounds. The bench was to have been composed of three persons commissioned by the governor, from six nominated by the house.

As this bill is not to be found in any of the editions of our laws, the natural presumption is that it never became one; a supposition, which the anger of the governor at the loss of one of the branches of his power, renders more than probable. In his message to the house of the 17th February, he declares his aversion to the bill, and complains of its unreasonableness in endeavouring to deprive him of one of his undoubted privileges, the free and unrestricted appointment of judicial offices.*

The contests between the governors and colonists in relation to courts of equity, here ceased; and the courts of law perceiving the hopelessness of a re-establishment of chancery, sedulously and laudably applied themselves to the remedying of this defect by a liberal administration of the common law.† They were steadily pursuing this course, when the great æra of the revolution arrived, which at the same time that it gave a new turn to other branches of the government, appeared to promise an extensive change in the judicial department.

* 3 Votes of Assembly, 269.

† Swift-*v*-Hawkins, 1 Dall. 17.

In the year 1776, the congress of the united colonies having declared them independent states, by a manifesto recommended that conventions should be called to settle their respective governments upon a new and republican footing.* This suggestion was acted upon in Pennsylvania within the same month, and of course the advantages of the introduction of chancery were considered. Of the proceedings of this convention, their various projects for the improvement of the judiciary, and the modes in which they were disposed of, no particular account remains at this day; the journal was never published, and the newspapers of the time are perfectly silent; nothing is now accessible from which we can form the least idea of what was proposed, but their final determination. In the 24th section, they gave to the courts the powers of a court of chancery, so far as related to the perpetuation of testimony, the obtaining of evidence from places not within the state, and the care of the persons and property of non-compotes; the section then concludes in these words; "and such other powers as may be found necessary by future general assemblies, not inconsistent with the constitution."†

The year 1790 is the true point at which we must fix the establishment of Pennsylvania jurisprudence. The constitution of '76, was framed at a time of popular commotion, of the successful termination of which, few were sanguine, and when even the city in which the convention sat was far from being secure. There

* Life of Franklin, by his grandson, p. 367.

† Minutes of the Convention of 1790. p. 19.

was no model approved by experience, after which it could be formed, and the whole was but an experiment in the art of government. It is not therefore surprising, that fourteen years afterwards, when the contest was at an end, and time, which developes the weakness of all structures, had shown the faults of this, it was deemed necessary to call a new convention in order to correct it in some of its most important branches.

By a body of which some of the most eminent lawyers of the state were members, it may easily be supposed that equity was not forgotten. In the draught of an amended constitution presented by the committee,* a court of chancery with all its powers and prerogatives was declared to be a branch of the judiciary, and a chancellor proposed, who, in addition to his judicial authority, was to preside in the senate during the trial of impeachments.† A lesser court of chancery was to be established in each circuit of the state, except that in which the superior court statedly sat, over which the president of the court of common pleas was to preside, with the title of chancellor of the circuit.‡ An appeal from his decrees, whether interlocutory or final, was reserved to the chancellor of the commonwealth.§

But the temper of the day was not such as to admit of so great and important an alteration in the judicial department. Our ancestors had retired from the war

* Messrs. Findley, Hand, Miller, Wilson, Irvine, Lewis, Jas. Ross and Addison.—Minutes of Convention, 38.

† Minutes of Convention. p. 42.

‡ Ibidem, p. 43.

§ Ibidem, p. 44.

of the revolution, with a bitter animosity to every thing that savoured of unusual power; and a proposition of this nature which tended to the introduction of an authority out of the ordinary course of law, was jealously and coldly received. When it was ascertained, that the convention would not adopt the proposition of a court of chancery, several modes were suggested, moderating the authority granted by the first, and softening its harshest features, so as to render it more agreeable to the people:* but all attempts were unsuccessful; and notwithstanding the strenuous exertions of the partisans of chancery, its powers were left in the same state, and almost in the same words as by the constitution of '76. The only difference consists in the change of the concluding sentence before-mentioned, for the following: "And the legislature shall vest in the said courts, such other powers to grant relief in equity, as shall be found necessary; and may from time to time enlarge or diminish those powers, or vest them in such *other courts*, as they shall judge proper for the due administration of justice."† This alteration was unquestionably made in order to give room for the establishment of a separate court of equity.

From that day until the present, though the subject has been frequently started, no alteration of importance has been made in the system.‡ A few new powers have been granted, by which the means of relief pos-

* Minutes of the committee of the whole convention, pages 56 and 70-1.

† Article V. Section sixth, Constitution, '90.

‡ Opinions of Provost of L. A. Book A. 112. 3 Griffith's Law Register, 244.

sessed by the courts were extended; but our jurisprudence itself in its most important features, remains almost the same. What these additions are, and the extent of their remedial effects, will be discussed with more propriety in a future branch of this dissertation.

Having thus traced the history of equity in Pennsylvania, from its settlement as a province, until the present day, it is now necessary that I should venture upon a delineation of its actual condition.

The subject of equity naturally divides itself into two branches; 1st, The principles, by which we understand the rules introduced by the court of chancery, for the government of its decrees; and 2d, The special powers by which courts of equity are enabled to do justice in cases for which the common law had not, or had inadequately provided, and which in legal language, are termed chancery powers.

The equity introduced into Pennsylvania consists,—as we have already seen,—in the adoption of the settled principles of the court of chancery, and their incorporation with the law itself. Our law is therefore now, to a great extent, what the common law of England would have been, had the judges accommodated themselves to the successive exigencies of the times, and by a skilful use of the malleable nature of the system, given to it that refinement and polish, of which it is more susceptible than any other body of jurisprudence.* Nor was it necessary, in attaining this end, to exceed the usual bounds of judicial authority; they had but to

* Du Ponceau on Jurisdiction, 17.

revert to the point at which their predecessors in England stopped, and by an exercise of liberality to perform that, which the latter in their strictness had refused. There are to be found in the common law itself, not only the necessary principles of equity and substantial justice, but even adequate forms for carrying them into effect.— They were not therefore called upon to usurp legislative powers, but to bring into full and fair action those which were already in existence.

To declare that there never will be a court of chancery in Pennsylvania, would probably be a bold, though certainly not an entirely unwarranted prediction; since from the first settlement of the country, to the present day, there has uniformly been a strong popular feeling in opposition to its introduction. In addition to this obstacle, there is *perhaps* a constitutional difficulty to be removed, before a court of chancery modelled upon that of England, and enjoying the same powers and prerogatives, can be established. The sixth section of the fifth article has empowered the legislature to vest equity powers in such courts as may be found necessary: but in the ninth article there is a provision, "that the trial by jury shall be as *heretofore*, and the right thereof shall remain inviolate." In the case of conflicting laws, the proper mode of ascertaining their true intent is to construe the one by the other in such a manner, if possible, that both may stand; using this method, the natural deduction in the present instance seems to be, that although the legislature may establish a court of equity, yet, that court must proceed by jury; and the chancellor cannot as in England, be a judge as well of the facts as of the law.

At the very threshold of the consideration of the mixed system, which has been substituted in Pennsylvania in lieu of the chancery powers, we are met by the important question of the policy of the union of law and of equity in the same jurisdiction. This point has been frequently agitated, and has caused much difference of opinion. The learned Bacon, who flourished when courts of equity were in their infancy, and when their powers first began to grow formidable to those of law, gives his opinion for the separation. "Apud nonnullos, receptum est, ut jurisdictio, quæ decernit secundum æquum et bonum, atque illa altera, quæ procedit secundum jus strictum, iisdem curiis deputentur; apud alios, autem ut diversis; omnino placet curiarum separatio. Neque enim conservabitur distinctio casuum, si fiat commixtio jurisdictionum: sed arbitrium legem tandem trahet,"* The authority of Bacon is certainly of the highest class; yet it must be considered that he was a great admirer of the Roman system of jurisprudence, the only one which in his day was known to have reached any high degree of perfection. The common law, by falling into the hands of subtle dialecticians, had become an artificial science, and Westminster Hall a school for subtle disputation; the liberality which it has attained in modern times could not be then foreseen, and a court proceeding according to the civil law, was probably in his opinion, the means best calculated to remedy the growing evil. Experience has now fully proved that equity and law can be concurrently administered by the same judges; and that when a sys-

* De Aug. Sciént l. 8. cap. 3. Aphorism, 45.

tem of jurisprudence is founded upon rational principles, and free from useless niceties, there is little more required to do complete equity, than a fair and correct interpretation of the law itself.*

I can conceive no substantial, or unanswerable reason against an union of the two jurisdictions; originally, that of equity began where the common law ended, or at least, where the common lawyers supposed it to end; and surely the same court which established the general rule, could in extraordinary cases, without incompatibility, regulate the exceptions. The argument of Lord Bacon is, that the bounds of equity and law should be kept distinct and separate; but time has shown, that although there may be a separation of courts, the jurisdictions may, and will eventually encroach upon each other. There are many cases in which the courts of law, fearful lest too much of their business should fall into the hands of courts of equity, have relaxed their ancient rigour, and will now entertain an action, although they formerly refused to grant relief, and thus drove the suitor into chancery; while at the same time, the courts of equity have preserved the jurisdiction, which was once exclusively vested in them, in consequence of the dereliction of their present competitors;† the result of which might be the very colli-

* Many eminent modern writers have considered a separation of the two jurisdictions at least useless, if not improper. I am indebted to Kames, Butler, and Wilson, for some of the arguments upon this subject.

† Atkinson-*v*-Leonard. 3 Brown's Chancery Reports, 224. 1 Fonblanque's Equity, 16.

sion which Bacon proposed to avoid by a separation of the courts. There can be no possible disadvantage in these modern times, in expounding the law by the rules of reason and natural justice; and this is attained by the union of the two powers in one tribunal.

In the early stages of the court of chancery, it was the custom before the complaint was heard, to send the party to law, in order to test the insufficiency of the ordinary rules to grant him relief,* and the regular consequence was a double expense and a double delay. In the time of Lord Cowper, this custom where the inadequacy of law was obvious, fell into disuse.† But still, even under the improved practice of the present day, a double suit is frequently necessary: for when the facts are complicated and uncertain, the chancellor, under a feigned issue, will send them to be investigated at law in order to obtain the benefit of an oral examination of witnesses, and a trial by jury.‡ If the case be mixed up of law and equity, the former is frequently referred

* 1 Fonblanque's Equity, 35. The humility of the court of chancery, in the first stages of its progress, stands in striking relief with the boldness it exhibits now that its jurisdiction has acquired a solid foundation. *Formerly* it allowed the judges of the common law to decide upon the propriety of the interference of equity: *now* it will not even permit a decision upon the propriety of their *own* interference. An injunction will restrain them whenever, in the opinion of the chancellor, they are exceeding their jurisdiction, by taking cognisance of matters of *conscience.*

† Butler's Reminisc. 44.

‡ 3 Bl. Com. 452.

to the judges,*—the several parts are tried before different tribunals,—two kinds of evidence must be given—and the pleadings themselves must be separate and distinct.

A separation imposes upon the suitor the decision of an important preliminary question, whether it is most fit and advantageous that his cause should be submitted to a court of law, or to one of equity? If he come to a wrong conclusion upon this point, he incurs, if not a loss of justice, at least a heavy penalty in costs. In addition to this disadvantage, it may be made the instrument of fraud by a plaintiff, who is aware that the defence of his adversary rests upon equity only. An action brought in a court of law deprives the defendant of his answer, and compels a tribunal erected for the purposes of justice, to pronounce an unjust and iniquitous sentence; the possible result is an execution, which, by impoverishing the defendant, prevents him from seeking his equitable relief in the halls of the chancellor.

It is of the utmost importance to a well regulated judiciary, that the scales of justice should be even and regular; and yet when there is a court of equity distinct from those of law, the measure of right will depend upon the jurisdiction, to which the application is made. In one of these courts, the decision must be unjust; for justice is an exact standard, add to it, or take from it, it will cease to be justice. The principles of equity are in some instances to be preferred to the rules of the common law; while in others, the latter are to be pre-

* 3 Bl. Com. 453.

ferred to the former; a court which can apply to each case the rules most conducive to the ends of justice, attains our idea of perfection in a judicial establishment.

This distinction of courts was an institution peculiar to England;* and it would be an error to suppose it the the result of a wise or profound combination. It was the offspring of a connexion of favouring accidents, such as never was presented by any other age or country, and which generated peculiar necessities. The sullenness of the common lawyers, the invention of uses, the liberality of the clerical chancellors, the favour of succeeding princes, all conspired together to elevate this new jurisdiction from a degree of insignificance, to an important and independent situation.† The court of chancery was originally but a college of scribes, over whom the king's secretary presided, performing a subservient duty to the courts of common law, in framing new writs, whenever they were necessary in the course of the administration of justice.‡ When the power of the ancient monarchs to mitigate the severity of the law devolved upon the chancellor, the cases in which he

* Mitford's Treatise, p. 1.—Butler's Reminisc. 45.—3 Bl. Com. 50.

† 1 Bohun's Curs. Cancel. 3.

‡ The oath of the chancellor was only that he would not sell, delay, or deny a remedial writ. 1 Roll. 384. Cancellario associentur, clerici honesti et circumspecti, domino regi jurati, qui in legibus et consuetudinibus Anglicanis, notitiam habeant pleniorem, quorum officium sit, supplicationes, et querelas consequentium audire et examinare, et eis, super qualitatibus injuriarum ostendere, debitum remedium exhibere, per brevia regis.—Fleta lib. 2. c. 12. 2 Inst. 407.

could interfere were circumscribed within extremely narrow boundaries,* and nothing but the ambitious character of the churchmen of that period, assisted by the remarkable revolution in the conveyance of property which occurred in the reign of Edward the Third, could have extended the jurisdiction of the court beyond its limited sphere, and elevated it into a rival of its ancient masters.†

In every nation of whose judicial system we have a tolerable account, equity and law are united in the same tribunal. The Roman prætor, the parliaments of France, the court of session in Scotland, and the court of conscience in Portugal, administered as well the strict law as its equitable interpretation. Throughout continental Eu-

* The most remarkable instance of that illiberality of the common law judges of early times, which rendered a new court absolutely necessary, is to be found in the construction they placed upon the penalty of a bond. Although it was obvious, that the sole intent of this clause was to evade the monkish objections to interest, and that provided the principal was paid with a proper compensation for the use, the plaintiff had no just cause of complaint, yet the courts of law, with an utter disregard to the first principles of justice, persisted in exacting the full amount of the penalty. Sir Thomas Moore summoned the judges to a conference, and counselled them to soften their strict rules; when this was obstinately refused, the chancellor, forgetting the gravity of his character, swore *by the body of God*, that he would grant an injunction in all such cases to stay their proceedings. (Wyllie-*v*-Wilkes Douglas, 505.) The statute of 4 & 5 Anne, c. 16, which remedied this injustice, did not extend to Pennsylvania; but our judges, with a spirit worthy of Mansfield, embodied it with the law.

† Dyversite des Cours, tit, Chancery, fol. 296.

rope distinct prætorian courts have either ceased to be in use, or have never been introduced. In our own country, the wisdom and policy of a division have been questioned; as notwithstanding the close resemblance which in other respects, our institutions bear to those of England, but eight of the twenty-four independent communities,* have drawn even partially the line of distinction between courts of law and equity. The constitutions of six of these were framed at an early date, when all our ideas of jurisprudence were borrowed from England. In the remaining sixteen they are blended together, though with various forms, and dissimilar bounds and regulations:†

That inconvenience has been suffered in England, in consequence of the separation of the two jurisdictions, and the necessary clashing of principles and judgments, is a fact too clear to require close investigation. In many instances, courts of law have full concurrent authority with those of equity, and their judgments when such points are presented to them, ought to have a conclusive effect. But so evident and proper a regulation, which should have been adopted at least through the respect which one court of justice owes to the decision of another, in matters within its jurisdiction, has

* New York, 3 Griffith's Law Register, p. 127.—New Jersey, 4 Griffith's L. R. p. 1180.—Delaware, 4 Griffith's L. R. p. 1030.—Maryland, 4 Griffith's L. R. p. 905.—Virginia, 3 Griffith's L. R. p. 321.—South Carolina, 4 Griffith's L. R. p. 829. —Missouri, 4 Griffith's L. R. p. 602.—Mississippi, 4 Griffith's L. R. p. 658.

† At the close of this dissertation, I propose to insert a brief sketch of equity, as it exists in our sister states.

not obtained in chancery; and cases may be found in which after the point had been formally decided at law, it has been made the subject of subsequent discussion, and contrary determination in the court of equity.*—The necessary result is a doubt and uncertainty, intolerable in any system of jurisprudence, and which prove plainly, that while the powers of law and equity are vested in unconnected tribunals, suitors are subject to two distinct codes, and liable to judgments as various as the natures of the courts.

With the union of law and equity in the courts of Pennsylvania, we have therefore reason to be satisfied; let us now recur to the system as it exists.

So early as the year 1684, equity was considered as a branch of the law of Pennsylvania, and as we have already seen, provision was made for the administration of justice, according to its principles. Though the chancery powers of our courts, from that time to the formation of the constitution, were in a continual state of fluctuation, yet the rules of decision remained constantly the same; and the first reports of our adjudged cases recognise equity as a branch of the law.

In Swift-*v*-Hawkins,† a case decided in 1768, Chief Justice Allen said that during the thirty-nine years of his recollection, (1727,) it had always been the practice in Pennsylvania under the plea of payment, to allow such a defence to be made as would be sufficient to discharge the party in a court of equity.

* See Greathead-*v*-Bromley, 7 T. R. 455, and the contrary decision of the chancellor, in 7 Ves. 3.

† 1 Dall. Rep. 17.

But the leading case upon this point is that of Pollard-*v*-Shafer.* In the course of his learned and elaborate opinion, Chief Justice M'Kean frequently declares that equity is a part of the law; and that wherever a case of that nature came within the cognisance of the courts, they would decide according to its principles, to prevent the failure of justice, which would otherwise arise from the want of a court of chancery. Accordingly, although the common law was supposed to lean strongly against the defendant, yet his plea, founded on equity only, was sustained upon a demurrer.

The law, as laid down in this case, has never been disputed, and all subsequent decisions have rested upon it as a secure foundation. In Wikoff-*v*-Coxe,† the supreme court said that "*unquestionably*" equity was a part of our legal system, and that parties were here allowed to make a defence that would be inadmissible at common law; and lastly, (for it is useless to recapitulate all the cases upon this point,) in Ebert-*v*-Wood,‡ the judges declined hearing the argument of Mr. Ross, stating that it was their settled practice to proceed upon the principles of equity.§

As these cases contain in themselves no restrictions,

* 1 Dall. Rep. 211, 213, 214,

† 1 Yeates' Rep. 358.

‡ 1 Binney's Rep. 217.

§ For other cases, see Wharton-*v*-Morris, 1 Dall. 125.—Stouffer-*v*-Coleman, 1 Yeates, 399.—Dorrow-*v*-Kelly, 1 Dall. 144.—Minsker-*v*-Robinson, 2 Yeates, 346.—Stansbury-*v*-Marks, 4 Dall. 130.—Murray-*v*-Williamson, 3 Bin. 138.—Jordan-*v*-Cooper, 3 Serg. & R. 578. 589.—Cope-*v*-Smith's Ex'rs. 8 Serg. & R. 115.

and have set this point completely at rest, the foundation of our equitable system is completely established. But now a difficulty naturally arises: the courts of Pennsylvania are courts of common law, proceeding according to its forms, and invested, with a few exceptions, solely with its powers; how are they then to administer equity, which is in so many cases opposed to law, and in general, requires processes so extremely different? The operation of this obstacle necessarily causes a restriction of the general rule, and equity may be described to be only so far a part of the law of Pennsylvania, as it can be brought within the cognisance of the ordinary courts, through the medium of the usual legal forms; except where the legislature have otherwise specially provided. With this limitation, the courts consider themselves bound in all cases to administer equity.*

The jurisprudence of Pennsylvania is thus changed in a very important particular. Its foundation is not the common law of England, in its restricted sense, but the common law incorporated with equity, mitigated in every instance by the principles of the latter, and thus adapted to the necessities of the time and country. It is a new system of obligations, compounded of the two, capable with a few additions, of uniting their excellencies, and administered by one tribunal. Law is tempered by equity, while equity itself, that luxuriant principle, whose ramifications it is so difficult to restrain, acquires by the union the steadiness of law.

At first glance, this difficulty in the way of the admin-

* Cope-*v*-Smith's Ex'rs. 8 Serg. & R. 115.

istration of equity, if not insuperable, would appear, at least, to restrict it within narrow bounds, and to extraordinary cases; but the liberality of the courts has done much to surmount the obstacle; and a continuation of the same line of conduct, together with a proper and frequent use of the means already provided, will in the end completely overcome it.

To systematize these modes introduced by the liberality of the courts, to pursue them to their consequences, and to deduce general rules for the government of future cases, are the principal ends of this dissertation. I will examine these points under two heads; 1st, The forms of adducing the equity of a plaintiff; and 2d, The modes by which an equitable defence has been made available. These two divisions will embrace all the cases decided in Pennsylvania, upon the principles of equity.

EQUITY OF A PLAINTIFF.

1. A declaration in an English court of law must contain all those points which the law considers necessary, in order to authorise a recovery;* a failure in this respect, and consequently a statement of facts which constitute only an equitable right, would be a sufficient cause of demurrer. Where there is a court of chancery, to which a plaintiff may have recourse in a difficulty of this nature, the rigour of one of the branches of the judiciary may be tolerated, since no irreparable injury can ensue: but where such a court has no existence, justice, the want of which, cannot be suffered in any

* 1 Chitty's Pleadings, 248.

system of jurisprudence, requires at their hands a relaxation in this particular. The courts of Pennsylvania early perceived the necessity for permitting the rule of the common law to be inflected; and the cases upon this point, few as they are in number, establish an important principle, which when time has more fully developed it, will have a powerful effect upon our systems both of law and equity.

The rule to which I refer, is that a right, merely equitable, may be made the ground-work of a recovery in our courts of common law; and when the claim is of this nature, the declaration is to be considered in the light of a bill in equity.

The first instance in which this innovation appears to have been permitted, was in the case of the Commonwealth *v*-Coates,* decided in 1791. In an action upon a bond or other sealed instrument, the common law in its ancient strictness, made a *profert* absolutely necessary; so that if the security were lost or destroyed, on prayer of *oyer*, the plaintiff must regularly have been non-suited.† The court of chancery only, could render adequate justice, by compelling a discovery from the defendant, and granting relief upon it.‡ In Pennsylvania, therefore, a party who lost his security, lost at the same time, according to the legal rule, the debt of

* 1 Yeates' Reports, 2.

† Leyfield's case, 10 Rep. 92 a. Co. Litt. 35 b. In Read-*v*-Brookman, 3 T. R. 151, the court of king's bench, in England. in opposition to the ancient authorities, sustained a declaration. stating that the bond had been lost by time and accident.

‡ Whitfield-*v*-Fausset, 1 Vez. 393. Anon. 2 Atk. 61.

which it was the evidence. So flagrant a defect of justice called loudly for a remedy; and in the case I have just mentioned, the court said, that on account of the want of chancery powers, the plaintiff, in lieu of a *profert,* might state specially, the cause which rendered it impossible.

The case of Lang-*v*-Keppelé,* was also decided upon the same principle. A suit for a partnership debt, at common law, must regularly be brought against the surviving partner; and the executors of the deceased, if sued, may plead in bar;† but a court of chancery, when the survivor is insolvent, or there is any other difficulty in the way of the remedy, will support a bill against the executors.‡ In Pennsylvania it was necessary that the rigour of the common law rule should be abated, and the equitable practice adopted; as otherwise, a creditor, notwithstanding his clear moral right, might have been deprived of all redress; the decision in Lang-*v*-Keppelé, was made upon this principle.§

But these cases are but instances of the application of

* 1 Binney's Rep. 123.

† Poston-*v*-Stanway, 5 East. 261.

‡ Lane-*v*-Williams, 2 Vern. 292.—Stephenson-*v*-Chiswell, 3 Vez. jr. 569.

§ The rule upon which the case of Lang-*v*-Keppelé was decided, had before been acted upon in Pennsylvania. In the year 1789, a judgment was obtained by Stephen Dutilh against Mason and Smith: as one of the defendants had died, and the survivor was insolvent, a *scire facias* was framed by Peter S. Du Ponceau, Esq. to compel the executors to show cause why an execution should not issue. Judgment was confessed to this writ without question of its legality.—1 Journ. of Jurisp. 248.

an invisible principle, whose action is no where even alluded to; and had they existed alone, the general rule with which I commenced this branch of the subject, could not without rashness, have been deduced. It was necessary to its complete and unquestionable establishment, that the case of Jordan-*v*-Cooper* should be decided, and that the judges should declare as they then did, its general applicability. Articles of agreement had been made for the sale of lands, and a deed was to have been delivered at a certain time; but as the vendor failed in the performance of this latter part of the contract, the vendee agreed by parol to accept the deed at a subsequent day, which he accordingly did. The purchase money being in arrear, the vendor brought an action of covenant in the usual form; but the supreme court held that it could not be supported, on account of the variance between the day of delivery mentioned in the agreement, and the time proved. But at the same time the judges declared, that by reciting the covenants, and afterwards stating in the manner of a bill in equity, the alterations which had been made by consent of parties, the difficulty could in future be obviated. The general principle, that equitable matter might be declared upon in Pennsylvania, and would constitute a sufficient ground of recovery, in cases coming within the like reason and necessity, was expressly asserted. Chief Justice Tilghman said, "There can be no doubt but equity would compel payment; but we have no court of equity.— What then is to be done? We may do as has been done

* 3 Serg. and Rawle, 564.

in other cases, where the forms of the common law were inadequate to the occasion; *we may frame a declaration, suited to the circumstances of the case.*"* A little farther, he says, "that equity is part of the law of Pennsylvania, has never been doubted; and that the defendant may put in a plea founded upon equity only, is equally clear. This was decided in the case of Pollard-*v*-Shafer (1 Dall. 210) in which the opinion of the court was delivered in a very powerful argument by Chief Justice M'Kean. If the defendant then may plead on principles of equity, why should not the same indulgence be extended to the plaintiff? We have never suffered ourselves to depart altogether from the forms of law; for I believe it has not been supposed, that our courts could take cognisance of a bill for the specific execution of an agreement. But when the object is to recover debt or damages, there is no reason why the usual form should not be somewhat relaxed, in order to reach the equity of the case. The propriety of so doing has long ago been perceived, and we are not without precedent to guide us."† The expressions of the other judges are equally strong and pointed,‡ and the rule stated at the commencement of this division, flows as a natural corollary.

It being thus clearly settled, that an equitable right may be made in Pennsylvania the subject of a recovery at common law, the mode of its enforcement now remains to be considered. From the nature of our

* 3 Serg. and Rawle, 578.

† Ibidem, 578-9.

‡ See more particularly p. 581.

courts, we are without the usual chancery executions, and the end of a suit must therefore be accomplished through the medium of *legal* process. If the equity of the plaintiff consist merely in a right to the receipt of a sum of money from the defendant, there is no necessity for an extraordinary intervention on the part of the court or jury, which should be granted sparingly, and only when the peculiar nature of the occasion would warrant it; but where the equity of the case calls not so much for a pecuniary compensation, as for the *performance of a certain act* by the defendant, it is necessary that they should advance one step farther, in order to render complete justice. This step is accomplished by granting conditional damages, so large in amount, that the defendant finds it to his advantage to yield to the plaintiff the equity which is the subject of the suit.

It is not to be supposed that this is a novel invention, arising from our peculiar necessities, and calculated only for the meridian of Pennsylvania. It is as ancient as the necessity for a court of chancery; and it was by an extension of its remedial effects, that Fairfax counselled his colleagues to check the progress of the clerical chancellors;* experience has now fully confirmed his claim to superior foresight and wisdom.

The first case, in which the reports show this mode to have been resorted to in Pennsylvania, was that of Clyde-*v*-Clyde,† decided in 1791. The plaintiff's right to a water-course had been maliciously disturbed by the

† Year Book, 21 Edw. 4. 23.

‡ 1 Yeates' Reports, 92.

defendant: the jury under the direction of the court, found large damages; the plaintiff's attorney having entered into an agreement to release them, in case of a proper and secure grant of the water-course.

The same remedy was given under precisely similar circumstances in an anonymous case,* and in Walker-*v*-Butz.† In Decamp-*v*-Feay,‡ the right to compel by this method, the specific performance of articles of agreement for the sale of lands, was admitted by the court. Other instances might be cited upon this point, if an enumeration of them were necessary;§ the general rule is fully established, that a defendant may be compelled to perform any act which equity would require of him, and which can possibly be enforced through the medium of an action sounding in damages. In this manner it supplies many of the chasms in the administration of justice, left by the want of a court of chancery, and is one of the most important and beneficial powers exercised by a court and jury.

There is one point to which special regard must be had, when a party seeks to avail himself of this power; for otherwise, instead of enforcing an equity, it might become an instrument of fraud. The jury must find the damages conditionally, at the same time prescribing the

* 4 Dall. Rep. 147.

† 1 Yeates' Rep. 575.

‡ 5 Serg. & R. 328.

§ Coolbaugh-*v*-Pierce, 8 Serg. & Rawle, 419.—Steigleman-*v* Wolfersberger, 5 Serg. & Rawle, 167.—Moody-*v*-Vandyke, 4 Binney, 43.—Kauffelt-*v*-Bower, 7 Serg. & Rawle, 81.—1 Smith's Laws, Note, 394.—Brackenridge's Law, Misc. 173.—3 Griffith's Law Register, 243.

terms on which they are to be released; for if the verdict be framed generally, though with a conditional intention, no court can prescribe the conditions of its enforcement, or declare the terms on which the compensation for the injury was made.*

II. Where one is seized of real estate to which another has an equitable right through the contract of the tenant, he is considered in chancery as a trustee to the use of the party out of possession;† the adoption of this principle by the courts of Pennsylvania constitutes the second mode of adducing the equity of a plaintiff. The difference between this form and the one I have just considered is extremely obvious. In the first, the declaration is an immediate application to the equitable powers of the court, stating like a bill in equity, all the circumstances that entitle the party to recover; while in this, a general count is made against the defendant, and it is only by evidence of the duty his conduct has imposed upon him, that the forms of the common law are made indirectly to assist and enforce the principles of equity.‡

The case of Stewart-*v*-Browne,§ is a strong instance of the operation of the chancery principle, through the medium of the common law form. The defendant had bought lands, at the sale of the Treasurer of the Commonwealth, under an agreement with the plaintiff, that

* Decamp-*v*-Feay, 5 Serg. and Rawle, 328.

† Green-*v*-Smith, 1 Atkins' Reports, 573.--Pollexfen-*v*-Moore, 3 Atkins' Reports, 273.

‡ Hawn-*v*-Norris, 4 Bin. 78.

§ 2 Sergeant & Rawle, 462.

the purchase when made should be for their mutual interest; Stewart was never in possession; but the court held that the agreement of Brown made him a trustee to the use of the plaintiff, as to one moiety, and consequently the action of partition was maintained against him.

But the flexible action of ejectment, that almost omnipotent creature of judicial ingenuity, is the most important and universal mode of enforcing the equity of a plaintiff, relating to land: wherever chancery will presume a trust to have arisen, and will compel its execution, the courts of Pennsylvania, proceeding according to this legal method, will grant the same relief.* The action of ejectment is, therefore, so far as relates to the principles which may arise upon it, the rules which are to guide it, and the ground-work of the judgment, precisely upon the footing of a bill in equity; and as any matter which would there constitute a right to the possession of land, is sufficient to support it,† the want of a court of chancery, is at least in this instance, completely supplied.

* A plaintiff in ejectment, in England, must be clothed with the legal title—Jones-*v*-Jones, 7 T. R. 43. 47. Da Costa-*v*-Wharton, 8 T. R. 2.—Blake-*v*-Luxton, 6 T. R. 289. So strict is the rule against equitable rights, that a trustee may support an ejectment against his own cestuy que trust—Reade-*v*-Reade, 8 T. R. 118, 123. Lord Mansfield appeared to be desirous of assuming through its medium a species of equitable jurisdiction; but all the cases decided by him, upon this principle, have long since been over-ruled. Adams on Ejectment, 33, 34.

† Peebles-*v*-Reading, 8 S. & R. 491. For other authorities see post. 53.

It was by following this principle through its extensive consequences and ramifications, that the courts were naturally led to an extraordinary addition to their chancery powers; no less than an authority to decree indirectly, the specific performance of a covenant. Cases must frequently occur, wherein from the deficiency of personal estate, or the peculiar circumstances of the parties, there could be no adequate relief, but an enforcement of the thing *in specie;* and according to the English distribution of judicial powers, this was only to be obtained in a court of chancery. As the legislature persisted in their resistance to the addition of such a branch to our judiciary, the courts of common law, mindful that it is the office of good judges to extend the means of rendering justice, sought for a method of accomplishing this desideratum to its administration. The stubborn and unbending forms of the ancient common law, rendered hopeless every endeavour to attain it through their medium; and recourse was therefore had to the more pliant and modern proceeding by action of ejectment.

The precise period when this alteration of the English law originated, unfortunately for the honour of its inventor, cannot at this day be ascertained; it has been used and approved of in Pennsylvania from time immemorial,* and is now too firmly rooted to be shaken by any power less than the legislature. It is a branch of our own common law, a custom arising from the necessities of the country, and its own intrinsic convenience.

The general rule relating to this use of the action of

* Hawn-*v*-Norris, 4 Bin. 78.

ejectment, shows conclusively its analogy with the chancery process. Wherever the chancellor in England will enforce articles of agreement, or decree a conveyance, the same relief will be granted in Pennsylvania, by our common law method.* Thus the vendee of lands by articles of agreement, who has completed his share of the contract, as by payment or tender of the purchase money, may by ejectment obtain possession, if withheld from him by the vendor.† His title is not a legal one, inasmuch as he has never had possession; but it is a claim in equity, which our courts will enforce, by an adoption of the chancery fiction, which is the ground-work of the bill for a specific performance,‡ that that shall be considered as done, which in equity and good conscience should have been done originally.§

The English statute of frauds and perjuries made a writing necessary, in order to transfer a right to land;

* Hawn-*v*-Norris, 4 Bin. 78.—Kauffelt-*v*-Bower, 7 Serg. & R. 81.—Peebles-*v*-Reading, 8 S. & R. 491.—M'Call-*v*-Lenox, 9 S. & R. 315.—Cope-*v*-Smith's Ex'rs. 8 S. & R. 115.—Griffith-*v*-Cochran, 5 Bin. 105.—Minsker-*v*-Robinson, 2 Yeates, 346.—Moody-*v*-Vandyke, 4 Bin. 41.—Vincent-*v*-Huff, 4 S. & R. 301, 2.—Willing-*v*-Brown, 7 S. & R. 469.—Riddle-*v*-Murphy, 7 S. & R. 236.—Coolbaugh-*v*-Pierce, 8 S. & R. 419.—Jones-*v*-Maffet, 5 S. & R. 528.—Collins-*v*-Rush, 7 S. & R. 155.—Stein-*v*-North, 3 Yeates, 327.—Campbell-*v*-Spencer, 2 Bin. 133.—Campbell-*v*-Sproat, 1 Yeates, 328. 1 Smith's Laws, Note 394.

† 4 Binney, 78. 5 Binney, 105. 8 S. & R. 115. 2 Yeates, 346.

‡ 1 Maddock's Chancery, 289. 1 Fonblanque's Equity, 419.

§ 4 Binney, 41. 3 S. & R. 585. 9 Serg. & Rawle, 315. 4 S. & R. 301. 8 S. & R. 115. 2 S. & R. 356. 8 S. & R. 25.

but the court of chancery regarding rather the equity, than the letter of the law, where part of a verbal agreement had been performed by the parties, would compel the completion of the remainder.* The Pennsylvanian act of 1772,† which is almost a transcript of the British statute, made the same requisition; and in consequence the courts still pursuing the analogy between the bill in equity and the action of ejectment, have adopted the chancery construction, and will grant the same relief.‡ The reasons of the English chancellors, 1st, that where the agreement has been acted upon, there can be no danger of perjury in proving it: and 2dly, that it is inequitable that any one should refuse to perfect a contract, from which he has derived advantage by a fulfilment in part, are mentioned by Chief Justice Tilghman, in the case of Ebert-*v*-Wood already referred to, and were concurred in by the whole court.§ For what will constitute such a part performance as to take the case out of the obligation of the act, we must therefore of course, resort to the reports of chancery decisions, and the rules there established.‖

The only substantial variation between the bill for

* 1 Maddock's Chancery, 300.

† 1 Smith's Laws, 389.

‡ Ebert-*v*-Wood, 1 Bin. 218.—Syler-*v*-Eckert, 1 Bin. 380.—Smith-*v*-Patton, 1 S. & R. 83-4.—Bassler-*v*-Niesly, 2 S. & R. 356.

§ 1 Binney's Reports, 218.

‖ It would enlarge this dissertation too much, to enter into a discussion of the English rules, relating to part performance. The subject is examined in 1 Maddock's Chan. 301, & 1 Fonblanque's Equity, 182.

the specific performance of an agreement in writing, or a parol contract in part performed, and the action of ejectment as used in Pennsylvania, consists therefore in the method of proceeding; the principles which govern them, and the species of relief, are precisely the same. Nor is this only difference to the disadvantage of our simple method. Though the principles of equity are enforced through the medium of common law process, yet the union far from generating a "hybridous monster without the virtues of either parent"* has created a mode, by which at the same time that the equitable principle is preserved, the superior promptness of the common law, and the simplicity of its forms, enhance the remedy and its advantages. Too much praise cannot be bestowed upon the inventors of this method for their ingenuity, nor too much gratitude for the important benefit they have conferred, by removing the obstacles that beset the way in Pennsylvania, of the proper administration of justice. They have enabled our judges to exercise permanently, a power which the profound Lord Hardwicke who spoke the words of wisdom,† declared to be the greatest and most useful head of chancery jurisdiction;‡ and this too, by a mode as beautiful as it is simple, as useful as it is ingenious.

Notwithstanding the extensive influence of this power, there is one instance in which we cannot, in Pennsylvania, compel the specific performance of a contract,

* Hoffman's Second Lecture, p. 34.

† So said Lord Mansfield and Mr. Burke; Butler's Reminisc. 130.

‡ Penn-*v*-Lord Baltimore, 1 Vez. 446.

through the medium of an ejectment, though this relief may be granted by the court of chancery, in England: this is where in his answer to a bill of discovery, the defendant, without relying upon the statute of frauds and perjuries for protection, confesses a parol agreement, of which no part has been performed.* As this proceeding arises from the peculiar organization of chancery, and the nature of its modes of proceeding, which compel the defendant to place his contract in writing, and to disclose the unconscientiousness of his refusal, it cannot here be resorted to; while on the other hand, the act of assembly of 1772,† prevents the operation of the action of ejectment, where there is no writing on which to ground it. But though the use of the English method is prohibited to us, we possess a mode peculiarly Pennsylvanian, which is equally beneficial in its relief, and less liable to uncertainty. The fourth section of the statute of frauds and perjuries, which provides against the recovery of damages on a parol contract, for the sale of lands, is entirely omitted in the act of assembly, though in other respects, the latter is a *verbatim* copy of the former;‡ the consequence is that an action for damages may be brought upon a parol agreement, of which no part has been performed,§ and where the refusal of the defendant is inequitable or fraudulent, the

* Whether a defendant who has confessed the agreement, can in any case protect himself under the statute of frauds, is vexata quæstio. 1 Fonbl. Eq. 181. 1 Maddock's Chan. 305.

† 1 Smith's Laws, 389.

‡ Ewing-*v*-Tees, 1 Binney, 455.

§ Bell-*v*-Andrews, 4 Dall. 152.—Ewing-*v*-Tees, 1 Bin. 455.

jury may and ought, by finding a large conditional verdict, to compel him to a specific performance.*

Thus, by an ingenious and liberal use of our common law methods, a vendee, under any form, or evidence of contract, may obtain *possession* of the land, as amply and completely as a court of chancery could have given it. In order, however, to his better and more complete enjoyment of the property thus awarded to him, it was necessary that the vendor should be compelled to execute proper conveyances, and thus to place the party in the same situation in which he would have been but for the inequitable refusal to perform the agreement: to supply the defect of this chancery power, we must recur to the universal method, by conditional damages; which has accordingly been applied to a fulfilment of this just and salutary purpose.†

As the interference of the court and jury in these several cases, arises from a liberal view of justice and necessity, the rule of chancery, that he who seeks equity should do equity, is always strictly observed. When the purchase money has not been paid, the jury will frequently make its liquidation a condition of their verdict, in order to protect the defendant from the chance of a second litigation: and the same course will be pursued with any other equity possessed by the defendant,

* Collins-*v*-Rush, 7 S. & R. 155-6.—Brackenridge's Law Misc. 173.

† 1 Smith's Laws, Note. p. 394. 3 Griffith's Law Register. p. 243.

for which provision should be made, before the plaintiff is entitled to recover.*

III. The action of replevin, from the liberal construction it has received, has become in Pennsylvania, a mode of compelling the specific performance of a personal contract. It may be applied to every case in which goods in the possession of one man are claimed by another;† and no distinction is made between those instances in which there has been a wrongful deprivation of possession, and others, in which the controversy relates only to the title.‡

The concessions of William Penn,§ and the act of 1705,‖ by which it was intended to settle the law of replevin, had specially declared that the writ should issue only in the same cases as in England; and there its sole use is to remedy an illegality in a distress.¶ Its great extension in Pennsylvania, has therefore induced some of our ablest lawyers** to term the present practice a custom of our own, which grew up without the sanction of a law, and merely through its necessity and

* Moody-*v*-Vandyke, 4 Bin. 43.—Mathers-*v*-Akewright, 3 Bin. 94.—Nicholas-*v*-Steigleberger, 5 S. & R. 172.—Barde-*v*-Wilson, 3 Yeates, 149.

† Weaver-*v*-Lawrence, 1 Dall. 157.—Woods-*v*-Nixon, Addis. 134.—Stoughton-*v*-Rappalo, 3 S. & R. 562.—Shearick-*v*-Huber, 6 Bin. 3.

‡ MS. Opinions of Prov. of L. A. Book A. 102.

§ 16th Concession, 1 Gallow. L. 7.

‖ 1 Smith's Laws, 44.

¶ 3 Bl. Comm. 146.

** Woods-*v*-Nixon, Addis. 134.—Opinions of Prov. Book A. 102.—Weaver-*v*-Lawrence, 1 Dall. 157.

convenience. But, however gratifying it may be to our national pride, to believe, that of a restricted proceeding, we have made an extensive remedy, an examination of our claims will show them to be in some measure ill founded; and that although the ancient common law did not provide precisely the same remedy, yet its approaches were extremely near.

In the early periods of the legal history of England, there were two kinds of replevin; the one in the *detinet*, the other in the *detinuit*. The first, as its name imports, lay where the goods were still detained by the defendant; the other, which is the only proceeding now known in England, was used when possession had been delivered to the plaintiff by the sheriff.* These actions lay originally in every case in which goods were taken *tortiously* from the party:† but the practice appears to have been discontinued at an early day; since Lord Coke, who was an eminent antiquarian, treats replevin as merely a mode of remedying an illegal distress.‡ By an union of the action, in the *detinet*, with the extensive operation anciently allowed to it, we have a proceeding very similar to the practice in Pennsylvania: so that the improvement made by our judges, though still great, is far less than is commonly imagined; it consists only in dispensing with the necessity for a *tortious* taking.

* 1 Saunders' Rep. 347. b. N. 2.—1 Chitty's Pleading, 158.

† Bishop-*v*-Viscountess Montague, Cro. Eliz. 824.—1 Chitty's Pleading, 158.—Selwyn's Nisi Prius, p. 1006. Note 2.

‡ Co. Litt. 145. b.—In 12 Coke's Rep. 79. tit. Admiralty, mention is made of the replevin of a *ship*, in the reign of Edward I.

As a natural consequence, however, of this improvement, the specific performance of a contract for the personalty, may in many instances be enforced; and a very brief consideration of these will show that they embrace every case in which the same relief could be obtained through the intervention of the court of chancery.

In every instance of articles of agreement for the sale of real estate, unless the case has in it something peculiar, a specific performance should be compelled; because as the purchase of lands arises from a particular preference, and no two estates combining precisely the same advantages can be found, adequate justice could not otherwise be rendered.* But when we endeavour to apply the same principle to chattels, we find the reason which operated in the case of lands, to have entirely ceased. Stock and merchandise of the same kind, may always easily be found and bought; and a complete compensation may consequently be made in damages, and obtained with greater promptness, through the medium of the forms of the common law. The court of chancery observing this distinction, will only extend the remedy so far as the reason will warrant; and therefore a mere contract for stock or merchandise, without any remarkable feature, will not be enforced;† though it is otherwise with an agreement for a valuable relic, family plate, or any other thing possessing a *pretium affectionis*, or quality peculiar to itself: for in those instances a proper relief could not otherwise be granted.

* 1 Maddock's Chan. 296.

† Cud-*v*-Rutter, 1 P. Wms. 570.—Buxton-*v*-Lister, 3 Atk 383.

The action of replevin will not only cover those cases in which the court of chancery will interfere, but in some instances is even more extensively remedial. Not only may family pictures be obtained,* for which an agreement has been made, but even merchandise, when the particular bales contracted for can be distinguished. Nor is the party replevying restricted as the complainant in the English court of chancery is, to the continuance of the possession of the defendant: he may follow the property through successive transfers, and as the doctrine of market overt has been adjudged not to hold Pennsylvania, he may replevy it, wherever it is found.†

In order to maintain this action, there must of course, be a right of property, or possession in the plaintiff; but the necessities and conveniences of commerce have so beneficially extended the acts by which the former may be vested, that but few agreements can be made without immediately conveying it. Marking the goods, packing them, or any other act evincing a former intention of delivery, will vest the legal right in the purchaser.‡

IV. When commerce had introduced frequent and necessary changes of property, many of the strict rules of the common law became inconvenient in practice, though founded upon what were anciently considered salutary principles. Of these there was none that called for more immediate correction and amendment than that which requires a privity, caused either by contract or

* Shearick-*v*-Huber, 6 Bin. 5.

† Hosack-*v*-Weaver, 1 Yeates, 478.—Hardy-*v*-Metzgar, 2 Yeates, 347.—Easton-*v*-Worthington, 5 S. & R. 130.

‡ Lickbarrow-*v*-Mason, 1 H. Bl. 363.

tort between the parties to an action. In the feodal ages, which gave birth to this principle, changes of property were unfrequent; and as they were generally accompanied by immediate delivery and payment, rights of action, viewed as positive interests, were too insignificant to attract the attention of the courts. It is not surprising, therefore, that it was considered a result of sound policy to prevent a transfer by their original possessor, "because under colour thereof, pretended titles might be granted to great men, whereby right might be trodden down, and the weak oppressed, which the common law forbiddeth."*

The progress of equity in England has been concurrent with that of commerce, strengthening with its strength, and growing with its growth. From the earliest period of their power, the principle of law has been deemed by the chancellors too absurd to be adopted;† for every rule should cease to exist with the reason that created it. In the liberal change that has been effected, they have led the way with so firm and unyielding a course, that but a single instance is to be found, in which there was a refusal to permit an assignee for a valuable consideration, to sue as fully and completely as his assignor.‡ Of this case it is proper to remark, that it occurred in the reign of James I. while the court of chancery was yet in its infancy, and long before its principles had acquired any degree of permanence or stability.

* Co. Litt. 214. a.

† Master-*v*-Miller, 4 T. R. 340.

‡ 11 James 1.--1 Roll. 376. I. 6.--Chitty on Bills, 4.--Bury-*v*-Hartman, 4 Serg. and Rawle, 184.

It was not until a very late day that any important progress was effected in the courts of law, although there are some vague expressions in the old reporters, which tend to show that the necessity for an abatement of this unseasonable rigour, was perceived at an early period.* The rule now is, that an assignee may maintain an action at law; and the court will exert itself to afford *every support and protection, not inconsistent with the established principles and modes of proceeding which govern tribunals acting according to the course of the common law.*† As a necessary consequence of this provision, the suit must be brought in the name of the assignor; and in this manner both the nominal and real plaintiffs are exposed to inequitable risks. The one to the payment of costs, when his interest in the subject matter has ceased; the other to evidence of the admissions of the plaintiff, and perhaps even to discontinuance.‡

In Pennsylvania, where there was no court of chancery to which recourse might be had, the judiciary have not testified this extreme reluctance to abandon a shadow after its substance had departed. By a simple but ingenious practice, which has prevailed from time immemorial,§ the strictness of the common law is evaded, and

* 12 Mod. 554.--1 Rol. Ab. 29.--Sid. 212.--T. Jones, 222.--4 T. R. 341.

† Welch-*v*-Mandeville, 1 Wheat. Rep. 236.—Master-*v*Miller, 4 T. R. 341, and cases there cited.

‡ The courts of New York have been very liberal in their decisions upon the right of the assignee of a *chose in action*. Johns. Dig. Assignment, II.

§ M'Cullum-*v*-Coxe, 1 Dall. 140.

the liberality of chancery completely introduced. The action, though brought in the name of him who is privy in law, is marked to the use of the party really interested; and throughout the whole procedure the latter is so completely regarded as plaintiff by the court, that they will suffer the suit to be brought without the consent of the former,* and will not permit him, in any case, to discontinue it.† If an attachment issue for costs, it must be against the assignee; and the assignor is a competent witness to the suit, as his interest is held to be totally divested.‡ By these means our courts have completely evaded the ancient, but now inconvenient requisition of privity; while by the same liberal proceeding they have given to the parties an application to the conscience of the assignor, who is in general the person best acquainted with the several facts and circumstances of the case.

The various decisions upon this point, in Pennsylvania, are all embraced in the few rules stated above: but it is evident, that a field is opened for many and important questions, which it is not fitting that I should endeavour to anticipate. Suffice it to say, that as the want of a court of chancery is declared to be the reason of this improvement of the common law,§ the principles of equity in relation to the rights and powers of the assignee, will probably in all cases be adopted.‖

* 3 Binney's Rep. 312.

† 1 Dall. 139.

‡ Steele-*v*-Phœnix Ins. Co. 3 Bin. 312.—Browne-*v*-Weir, 5 Serg. & R. 403.

§ 3 Bin. Rep. 312. 5 Serg. & Rawle, 403.

‖ Thus payment to the assignor, without notice of the assign-

By the civil law, *choses in action* were not assignable; but a fiction was soon framed by the jurisconsults, which gave the right of transferring a debt, without the consent of the debtor. The assignee was constituted the agent of the assignor, *(procurator in rem suam)* and could then bring a suit, which was regularly to be prosecuted at his own risk and expense.* It is pleasing to observe in two codes springing from distinct sources, the same progress arising from a similar spirit of liberality and improvement. It proves to us, that our science is the joint result of wisdom and experience; and discloses the nice links, which, according to Sir William Jones, connect the subordinate branches of one great system of jurisprudence.

With this head I conclude the common law methods, through whose intervention an equitable claim may be enforced.

ment, will discharge the debtor.—Brindle-*v*-M'Ilvaine, 9 S. & R. 77, and Bury-*v*-Hartman, 4 S. & R. 184. When the action is brought in the name of the assignor, generally, as there is a clear liability in him for the costs, it stands of course upon a different footing. But even in this case, if the trust be shown to the court, they will consider the assignee as the real plaintiff. Thus the defendant may name in his plea, the person to whose use the action is really brought, in order to avail himself of a set-off; or suggest his name on the record, to charge him with costs. Canby-*v*-Ridgway, 4 Bin. 496. If the assignee wish to make the assignor a competent witness, he must pay the whole amount of costs, into court, and in such case there is an implied condition that they shall in no event be returned to him.—North-*v*-Turner, 9 Serg. & Rawle, 249.—Conrad-*v*-Keyser, 5 Serg. & Rawle, 370.

* Pothier, Contrat de Vente, tome 1, s. 550.

EQUITABLE DEFENCES.

When the party who requires the assistance of equity is defendant, the manner of availing himself of its power, and resisting through its medium the demand of the plaintiff, is far more simple and universal than where a claim is to be supported. To attain this end, the forms of the common law required no unnatural extension or inflection; it was neither necessary to invent novelties, nor to revive practices which had long been forgotten; a love of justice and its consequence, liberality in the judges, were the only requisites, and fortunately these were qualities easily found upon the bench. The strictness of the rules of English pleading, opposed the only barrier to the admission of an equitable defence, as fully and generally as it would be permitted in the court of chancery: and attention was so early and successfully paid to a relaxation in this particular, that the period of the non-existence of the practice, which has ripened into common law, cannot now be ascertained.

A defendant in Pennsylvania, is permitted under certain general pleas, to give evidence of equitable matters foreign to their nature, and appertaining to a very different species of defence: or if this mode be inconvenient or improper in his particular case, he may plead specially his equitable right, and thus obtain the advantages of a chancery answer, so far as they relate to a complete statement of his case. The methods of asserting the equity of a defendant, therefore, naturally resolve themselves into two kinds: 1st, That in which the defence is made by evidence of equity, given under a general plea;

and 2dly, That in which the equitable ground is specially pleaded.

I. Of general pleas to a personal demand.

Payment.—The practice of giving in evidence under the plea of payment, matters relating to a defence, whose only foundation is equity, may be traced to the earliest stages of our jurisprudence, and is a branch of the common law that arose out of those peculiar wants of the province of Pennsylvania, to which I have already so frequently adverted.* The general rule adopted by the courts, is that whatever would be sufficient in chancery to protect the party, will be admitted in evidence, under the general plea of payment; and that shall be presumed to be *paid*, which in equity and good conscience, ought not to be *paid*.† The cases in our reports serve very fully to illustrate and prove this general principle, as they include almost every species of defence usually made in a court of chancery.

The various defences permitted in equity, may be classed under the heads of want of consideration, fraud, mistake and accident;‡ the equitable grounds specified

* Sparks-*v*-Garrigues, 1 Bin. 164.—Swift-*v*-Hawkins, 1 Dall. 17.

† Sparks-*v*-Garrigues, 1 Bin. 164.—Robinson-*v*-Eldridge, 10 Serg. & R. 142.—Cope-*v*-Smith's Ex'rs. 8 S. & R. 116.—Gochenauer-*v*-Cooper, 8 S. & R. 203.—Galbraith-*v*-Ankrim, 2 Browne, 120.—Hollingsworth-*v*-Ogle, 1 Dall. 260.—Griffith-*v*-Chew, 8 S. & R. 25.

‡ Sir Thomas Moore used to say that the following doggrel contained all the heads of chancery jurisdiction:

Three things are to be helpt in conscience,
Fraud, accident, and things of confidence.

in the rule of the supreme court, relating to the plea of payment, are the want of consideration, fraud, a suggestion of falsehood and a suppression of truth.* As order is an important requisite in a legal composition, I will disregard the two last, as being but varieties of the second, and add mistake and accident, which, although not included in the rule, are causes recognised by authorities, and make our equitable system agree with that of England.

1. *Want of consideration.*—When a contract is merely by parol and without consideration, the common law borrowing the phrase of the civilians, calls it *nudum pactum*, and it cannot be enforced in a court either of law or equity. But when the agreement is made by an obligation under seal, the binding force of the contract, even though there be no consideration, is materially altered. Every bond containing the *verba præscripta solemnia*, is an immediate gift in law, of the money, and imports from the deliberation with which it is supposed to be made, a sufficient consideration.† The consideration of a promissory note in the hands of an innocent indorsee, for the convenience of commerce, is not examinable either at law or equity,‡ but as it is only a simple contract agreement, a defence relying upon a want of reciprocity, will be admitted even in a court of common law, in a suit brought by the payee against the maker.§ It is therefore somewhat

* Rule 59th of the supreme court.

† Gilbert's Reports, 154.—Brown-*v*-Marsh, Harde. 200.—Plowden, 308.

‡ Gilbert's Lex Prætoria, 288.

§ 1 Comyn on Contracts, 12.

surprising that they have not extended the same rule to bonds, and that they still continue in every case to deem the seal of the obligor conclusive evidence of consideration. As the law is, relief can only be had in a court of chancery,* and that court will enforce the rules of equity both against the obligee of the bond and his assignee; since the right of the latter by assignment arises solely from an equitable provision.†

In Pennsylvania, the law relating to this point, has long been settled according to the principles of equity, in order to avoid the manifest injustice which would otherwise have ensued. In Swift-*v*-Hawkins,‡ the court said, that the want of consideration to a bond could be shown under the plea of payment, although in an English court of law, such a defence would not be permitted: and the same principle has been asserted in succeeding cases.§

An act of assembly,‖ passed in 1715, rendered bonds and promissory notes assignable at law, and gave the assignee a right of suit in his own name, independently of his assignor. A question then arose, whether these two instruments were not to be placed upon a similar footing, as to the effects of a transfer: so that evidence of want of consideration to a bond, would be restricted to suits between the original parties, in the same manner as with

* Wright-*v*-Moor, 1 Chan. Rep. 157.

† Turton-*v*-Benson, 2 Vern. 765.

‡ 1 Dallas' Reports, 17.

§ Baring-*v*-Shippen, 2 Bin. 166.—Bryson-*v*-Ker, 4 S. & R. 309.—Heck-*v*-Shener, 4 S. & R. 256.—Solomon-*v*-Kimmel, 5 Bin. 234.

‖ Smith's Laws, 90

promissory notes nnder the statute of 3 and 4 Ann. Cap. 9. In Baynton-*v*-Hughes,* the case in which this point was mooted, the court, observing the distinction between *assignability* and *negotiability,* decided that the assignee of a bond was here to be considered in the same light as in a court of chancery, and was liable to the equity of the obligor against the original obligee; the law has in consequence always been so held in Pennsylvania.†

2. *Fraud.*—That the fraud of a party who has obtained a bond either by a suggestion of falsehood, or a concealment of truth, may be given in evidence, under the general plea of payment, is a point so clearly settled by numerous authorities, that it will be only necessary that I should cite a few by way of examples.

In Baring-*v*-Shippen,‡ a bond had been obtained from the defendant, (a lady) by one Cutting, in order to raise money for her use; but being in embarrassed circumstances, he assigned it to the plaintiff as a security for his own private debts. The court held that under the plea of payment, the fraud might be given in evidence; and the defendant thus discharged herself from the obligation in the hands of the assignee.

In Carpenter-*v*-Groff,§ a case removed by writ of error into the supreme court, the plaintiff in error, in consequence of an oath taken by the defendant in a for-

* 1 Dallas' Reports, 23.

† Solomon-*v*-Kimmel, 5 Bin. 234.—Bury-*v*-Hartman, 4 Serg. & R. 177.

‡ 2 Binney's Reports, 154.

§ 5 Serg. & Rawle, 165.

mer judicial proceeding, had given a bond by way of compromise. The perjury of the plaintiff below, having been ascertained, the obligor refused to discharge the bond; and on suit brought, he offered under the plea of payment, to give evidence of the fraud. The testimony was rejected by the court of common pleas, but their decision was reversed in the supreme court.

As these cases are amply sufficient for the present purpose, and it is unnecessary to state specially others in which their authority is confirmed,* I will proceed to the third branch.

3. *Mistake and accident.*—The rule of the common law which directed the mode in which mistake in the execution of a bond should be pleaded, was extremely inequitable, and savoured strongly of the ignorance and barbarity of the early period at which it originated. A party who had executed an agreement contrary to his intention, was obliged to rely upon the plea of *layman and unlettered;*† so that on proof of his *ability to read,* a fraudulent plaintiff would be entitled to a recovery. The court of chancery proceeding upon broader principles of natural justice, would relieve a party wherever there was a plain mistake proved by irrefragable evidence.‡

* Heck-*v*-Shener, 4 S. & R. 256.—Robinson-*v*-Eldridge, 10 S. & R. 142.—Sparks-*v*-Garrigues, 1 Bin. 164.—Miller-*v*-Henderson, 10 Serg. & R. 292.

† Thoroughgood's case, 2 Rep. 96.—Pigot's case, 11 Rep. 27.—More, 184.—2 Freem. 194.

‡ Henkle-*v*-Royal Exchange Company, 1 Vez. 317.—Langley-*v*-Browne, 2 Atk. 195.

In Pennsylvania the equitable principle has been adopted, and the plea of payment is made the medium of its enforcement. In Swift-*v*-Hawkins,* Chief Justice Allen said that within the scope of his recollection, which extended as far back as the year 1727, this had always been the practice; and it has continued until the present day unimpaired, and without question or dispute.

In Galbraith-*v*-Ankrim,† the court said, "There can be no doubt of the principle, that in a suit on a bond in Pennsylvania, the defendant under the plea of payment, may prove *mistake* and want of consideration: and that in such case, the jury may and ought to presume every thing to have been paid, which *ex æquo et bono,* in equity and good conscience ought not to be paid."‡

As to the discharge of a party from an obligation, by an accident unforeseen at the time of its making, whenever such cases occur, the court will proceed upon the principles of equity, and will allow the facts to be given in evidence under the general plea of payment. In Solomon-*v*-Kimmel,§ Chief Justice Tilghman said that it had often been decided, that when a bond was given for the purchase money of land, to which the title afterwards proved to be defective, the obligee could not recover. The decision in Pollard-*v*-Shafer,‖ was grounded upon the principles of equity, relating to accidents;

* 1 Dallas' Reports, 17.

† 2 Browne's reports, 120.

‡ Murray-*v*-Williamson, 3 Bin. 308.—Baring-*v*-Shippen, 2 Bin. 154.

§ 5 Binney's Reports, 233

‖ 1 Dallas' Reports, 210.

and though this was not done under the plea of payment, on account of the particular nature of the action, (covenant,) yet it shows that those rules have been adopted, and that facts which constitute such a defence, may therefore be given in evidence under this equitable general issue.

There was one difficulty for which it was necessary to make provision, in order to prevent the means of enforcing equity from becoming the instrument of fraud. If the general plea of payment were alone to be put in, without any other explanation of the defendant's intentions, it is obvious from a view of the extensive varieties of defence, which the courts in their liberality will permit to be made, that he would possess a highly inequitable advantage over the plaintiff, who at the day of trial, might be surprised by an answer against which he had had no previous cause to provide. A perception of this injustice has induced the supreme court to make a rule requiring the defendant to give notice of the equitable matter which constitutes his true defence.*

If in his notice of an equitable defence, the defendant present a case in which a court of chancery would not relieve, the plaintiff may object to the evidence, and pray the opinion of the court without submitting the case to the jury. The court will then reject the evidence, either *in toto*, or partially, as insufficient and irrelevant.†

When the equity of the case is opened by the plea of

* Rule 59th of the supreme court. This rule obtains likewise in the district court. See Troubat and Haly's valuable Manual of Pennsylvania Practice, p. 131.

† Robinson-*v*-Eldridge, 10 Serg. and Rawle, 142.

payment, the plaintiff in his turn, under the replication of *non solvit*, may give evidence of such special matters as would rebut the defendant's equity in a court of chancery;* so that although the forms of the common law are the only means employed, yet the decisions of our courts, and the determination of the cause, are in such cases entirely and completely guided by the principles of equity.

Non assumpsit.—Thus as we have seen, through the liberal manner in which the forms of the common law have been moulded by the judiciary, any matter which would discharge the party in chancery from a personal claim, or would rebut his equity, may be given in evidence under the plea of payment, or the replication of *non solvit,* to the ordinary kinds of actions. In the case of Stansbury-*v*-Marks,† there appeared to be a disposition in the learned judge, who delivered the opinion of the court, to extend the plea of *non assumpsit,* in the same manner, so as to render similar justice. He said, "The evidence (of infancy) is clearly admissible. Under the general issue, however, the jury may decide, whether the evidence is sufficient to discharge him or not. The position is generally true, that an infant can only bind himself for necessaries; yet in the court of chancery cases occur, in which a payment would be decreed, contrary to the strict rule of the common law. In this form of action equity is the principal consideration; and

* M'Cutchen-*v*-Nigh, 10 S. & R. 344.—Jordan-*v*-Cooper, 3 Serg. & R. 589.

† 4 Dallas' Reports, 130.

from necessity the courts of law in Pennsylvania adopt the principles of the English courts of chancery."

Notwithstanding these favourable expressions, if a defendant intends to avail himself of a defence founded upon equity, it is most prudent to rely upon the plea of payment, which is the favourite equitable plea of the courts. The extension of *non assumpsit* to new cases, was severely reprobated by Chief Justice Tilghman, in Dunlap-*v*-Miles,* and the decision there made, may be considered as overruling that of Stansbury-*v*-Marks. "Whether a court of equity under such circumstances, would afford relief, there is no occasion *now* to determine; for the point is, was the evidence admissible or not, in a *court of law* under the plea of *non assumpsit.*" A little farther he says—"If the circumstances of the case afforded ground for relief in equity, Dunlap ought to have given notice of the special matters, in consequence of which, under our practice, he might have brought forward all his *equity* under the *plea of payment.* I am not for extending the admissibility of evidence under the plea of *non assumpsit.* It has been carried far enough, and in my opinion, much too far already: so far as to involve plaintiffs in difficulties on trials, without any possibility of knowing the matter on which defendants rest their defence." Mr. Justice Yeates said, "I have not the smallest difficulty in asserting, that on the general issue of *non assumpsit,* the (equitable) evidence, offered upon the trial, could not be received at *common law.*"

The general rule flows as a natural consequence from

* 4 Yeates' Reports, 370.

these several declarations, that under the issue formed by *non assumpsit*, the courts will consider themselves as courts of common law; and that in those actions to which the plea of payment applies, it is only through the medium of that plea that the principles of equity may be called into action.

SET-OFFS.—The great facility with which the equity of a defendant may be supported, even by the forms of the common law, has enabled the courts to adopt to *their full extent*, the equitable set-offs allowed by courts of chancery. There was nothing in the legal forms which presented the slightest obstacle to the admission of a defence of this nature. as fully as in a court of equity: and the judges of Pennsylvania, with their usual promptitude, availed themselves of the advantage thus presented to them.

The cases upon this point, though few, are full, and clearly establish the general principle. In Murray-*v*-Williamson,* the defendant was allowed to set-off against the demand of the plaintiff, under the plea of payment, a bond which had been informally assigned, so that there could be no recovery at law, though the demand was good in equity. In Waln-*v*-Bank of North America,† Mr. Justice Duncan, who delivered the opinion of the court, declared that they had admitted the rules of chancery relating to defalcations, in their fullest extent: and the general principle is repeated and confirmed in Gochenauer-*v*-Cooper.‡

* 3 Binney's Reports, 135.

† 8 Serg. & R. 88.

‡ 8 Serg. & R. 202.—See too Robinson-*v*-Beall, 3 Yeates, 267.

To those who are accustomed to a court of equity distinct from the common law jurisdiction, this mode of proceeding will appear to be loose and inconvenient; but as the practice is regulated in Pennsylvania, it possesses some important advantages, and is in no manner productive of surprise upon the plaintiff. When a defendant, under a general plea,* intends to defalk his equitable claim, he is compelled by a rule of court to give notice of his determination, together with a copy of the account upon which he intends to rely, otherwise it will not be admitted in evidence.† If the defalcation be specially pleaded, notice is of course unnecessary.‡ In this manner not only is complete justice rendered, but a multiplicity of suits is prevented. An English court of law being without this liberal mode of dispensing justice, would be obliged to give judgment for the plaintiff; while the defendant would be turned round to a second suit in chancery.

Performance.—It may be laid down as a principle, practically true, that from the intricacy and subtleties that attend the pleadings to the action of covenant, it possesses in the strictness of the common law, no general issue. The plea of *non infregit conventionem* has been adjudged bad on demurrer;§ and under that of *non*

* See Act of 1705, 1 Sm. Laws, 49.

† Wharton's Digest, 530.

‡ Commissioners of Berks county-*v*-Ross, 3 Binney, 539.—Jacks-*v*-Moore, 1 Yeates, 391.—Boyd-*v*-Thompson, 2 Yeates, 210.

§ 3 Wooddes' Lectures, 93.—1 Chitty's Pleadings, 481.—8 T. R. 278.

est factum, the defendant merely puts the deed in issue, and can only prove, either that he never made the agreement charged against him, or that from some legal disability, it was absolutely void.* Whenever, therefore, the defence of the party goes to a denial of the alleged breaches, it is necessary in England, to have recourse to special pleading.

The plea of *performance*, or *covenants performed*, though not unknown to the ancient common law, has long been obsolete in English practice in consequence of its limited applicability. Even at the time when this plea was in ordinary use, it was held to be a governing principle, that it could only be resorted to where the covenants were *affirmative:* if one of the articles of the agreement had been *negative or disjunctive*, the answer of the defendant was informal, and liable to a demurrer.† Restricted as this plea was, by the action of these nice distinctions, to an insignificant and narrow operation, it is not surprising that it fell into gradual disuse; and as the modern opinion appears to be that by reason of its generality, it is now in all cases insufficient,‡ it is no longer enumerated in the books of pleading.§

As in actions of *debt* and of *assumpsit*, the courts of Pennsylvania, by a series of liberal decisions, have made a particular plea the vehicle of equity, so by rescuing the plea of performance from the neglect into which it had fallen, and giving it a more general application,

* Stephen on Pleading, 174-6.—1 Chitty's Pleadings, 481.

† Bacon's Abridgment, tit. "Covenant." K.

‡ 3 Wooddes' Lectures, 93.—Sayer-*v*-Minns, Cowp. 575.

§ Stephen on Pleading, 174-6.—1 Chitty's Pleadings, 481

they have avoided the intricacies of special pleading, and extended the benefit of an equitable defence to actions of covenant. It is a well settled rule in our courts, that under this plea, aided by an informal notice, any matter may be given in evidence that would discharge the defendant in a court of chancery; and that shall be presumed to have been performed, which in equity and good conscience ought not to be performed. There could be no stronger assurance of the liberal disposition of the judiciary towards the plea of performance, than the fact that its effects and operation have been compared to those of the plea of payment.*

By this method, which is peculiarly Pennsylvanian, we possess the certainty of special pleading, without its dangers, and the principles of equity without the dilatoriness of its forms.

II. Of the general plea where the claim is to the realty.

As an equitable title may be made the foundation of an action of ejectment, and is sufficient to ground a recovery, it follows as a natural consequence that it may protect the actual possession of a defendant. From the nature of the various species of defence before enumerated, they are necessarily confined to those cases in which the demand is *personal;* where the claim is *real,* recourse must be had to other methods, in order to render available the equity possessed by the party.

The action of ejectment, from the great improvements it has received, and its peculiar advantages, is almost the

* Bender-*v*-Fromberger, 4 Dall. 439.—Neave-*v*-Jenkins, 2 Yeates, 108.

only method used in Pennsylvania to try a title to land.* Among other provisions made by acts of assembly,† to simplify its proceedings, it has been enacted that the general plea of "not guilty" shall be the only plea put in by the defendant; and the special nature of the defence can therefore only be given in evidence.

If the equity of the defendant be merely founded on the non-performance of a particular act by the plaintiff, such as the payment of purchase money,‡ or making title to a part of the land,§ it is always made a pre-requisite to the recovery of the possession of the land by the latter; and may be either relied on in the defence, or judgment will be arrested by the court until it is performed.‖ The pervading principle of chancery interference, that he who seeks equity should be compelled to do equity, was adopted by our courts when they extended their jurisdiction, for the better administration of justice.

When the equity of a defendant goes to a total denial of the title of the plaintiff, it is supported by a recurrence to the principle which forms the ground-work of the equitable action of ejectment, that every thing shall be presumed to be done, which in good conscience ought to have been done. If, therefore, the party ought to have received proper title deeds, he will be considered in the same situation as if they had been actually deliv-

* Morris-*v*-Vanderen, 1 Dall. 67.

† Act of 13th April, 1807, 4 Sm. Laws, 476.—Gallagher-*v*-M'Nutt, 3 S. & R. 409.

‡ Vide p. 53 antè.

§ Mathers-*v*-Akewright, 2 Bin. 93.

‖ Ibidem.

ered to him: and the same course will be pursued with every other equity to which he may be entitled.* In the establishment of these liberal regulations, the courts appear to have been actuated by the same spirit with the legislature, which so early as 1705, had enacted that a quiet possession of seven years under an *equitable* right, should give an unquestionable title to the land.†

III. Of special equitable pleas.

The last mode by which a defendant may avail himself of the assistance of equity, is when the facts of his case are specially pleaded.

The act of assembly, of which I have just spoken, which restricts the defendant in ejectment to the general plea of not guilty, necessarily deprives him of this mode of asserting his equity, and confines it in practice to those cases in which the demand is of a strictly personal nature. With this exception, wherever the pleas before enumerated would be inconvenient or improper, from the nature of the action, the defendant may state his equity specially, and the courts will support it as a sufficient defence. The general rule was established in Pollard-*v*-Shafer,‡ and has been recognised as law, by a number of succeeding decisions.§ In the former case the defendant pleaded at length, that a house which he had covenanted to keep in repair, had been destroyed

* Griffith-*v*-Cochrane, 5 Bin. 105.—M'Call-*v*-Lenox, 9 Serg. & Rawle, 315.

† 1 Smith's Laws, 48.

‡ 1 Dallas' Reports, 214.

§ Murray-*v*-Williamson, 3 Bin. 136.—Hartzell-*v*-Reiss. 1 Bin. 291.—Jordan-*v*-Cooper, 3 Serg. & Rawle. 578.

by the British army under General Howe, in 1777; and the court declaring that an enforcement would be inequitable, relieved him from his agreement.

The practice of pleading specially the equity of a defendant, possesses one of the most important advantages of the answer in chancery, in stating at length all the circumstances of the case, without regard to their intricacy or complication. But for this method, the operation of equity would be narrow and restricted: as the rule now is, it supplies all the chasms left by the general pleas, so that no case can possibly occur in which a defendant may not rely upon his equitable right, as fully and completely in a Pennsylvania court of law as in an English court of chancery.

Of the lien of judgments.—Equitable rights having thus by the liberality of the judiciary of Pennsylvania become vested and tangible interests at law, it was necessary to the complete attainment of justice, that the new advantage thus vested in the party should be attended with its corresponding burthens. Proceeding upon this just and natural principle, it has been decided in our courts, that every species of equitable right is subject to the lien of a judgment, and may be sold so fully and completely under an execution, that the sheriff's vendee will stand in precisely the same situation as the original defendant. This rule resulting from a connected series of decisions, is thus stated by Chief Justice Tilghman:* "By the law of Pennsylvania all the real estate of the debtor, whether legal or equitable, is

* Auwerter-*v*-Mathiot, 9 Serg. & R. 402.

bound by a judgment against him, and may be taken in execution, and sold for the satisfaction of the debt. At common law, an equitable estate is not bound by a judgment, or subject to an execution. But the creditor may have relief in chancery. We have no court of chancery, and have therefore from necessity established it as a principle, that both judgments and execution have an immediate operation on equitable estates."

As in the establishment of this rule, the courts were guided by the most liberal and enlightened views of relative justice, they have not suffered themselves to be deterred by any technical niceties, from its steady application. Though the province of an essay is rather to deduce general principles than to specify the particular instances of their application, yet I may be permitted to cite a few authorities, in order to show the liberality with which our judiciary have extended the liabilities of a debtor, to cases in which the want of a court of chancery would otherwise have been his protection.

In Carkuff-*v*-Anderson,* the right of pre-emption vested by law in the settlers of Luzerne county, under the pretended Connecticut title, was held liable to the lien of judgment.

In Ely-*v*-Beaumont,† the plaintiff in error had a leasehold estate with a condition that he might erect buildings upon the premises, and if at the expiration of the term, they were not paid for by the lessor at a sti-

* 3 Binney's Rep. 8.

† 5 Serg. & Rawle, 126.

pulated valuation, he might then hold them in fee simple. As buildings were erected accordingly, it was held that his interest ceased in equity to be a mere chattel real, and was subject to the lien of judgment.

In Richter-*v*-Selin,* the equitable right of a vendee by articles of agreement, was declared to be subject to a lien and to execution.

The general rule established by these and other cases,† that every *beneficial equitable interest* is subject in Pennsylvania to execution under common law process, must as a necessary consequence of the nature of our judiciary be restricted to those special branches of equity which are cognisable through the medium of the ordinary legal forms. All other claims are of course incapable of *remedy*, and can never, therefore, be admitted as *rights* by the judiciary.

From this general view of the modes by which a party, whether plaintiff or defendant, may adduce his equity through the medium of legal forms, it may properly be inferred, that a court of law in Pennsylvania, is at the same time, a limited court of equity;‡ and that justice will be administered upon equitable principles, so far as the powers of the court, derived from the common law, will admit of this extension. The cause in its several parts must follow the legal rules: but if the principles of equity can incidentally arise, without re-

* 8 Sergeant & Rawle, 440.

† Vandevender's case, 2 Browne, 308.—Semple-*v*-Burd, 7 S. & R. 289.—Foust-*v*-Foster, 2 Serg. & R. 13.

‡ Cope-*v*-Smith's Executors, 8 S. & R. 116.

quiring a variation from the ordinary forms, the judgment will be framed upon their foundation.

The case of Yohe-*v*-Barnet's administrators,* in which it was decided that the courts of Pennsylvania could not in certain cases, insist upon a provision for a wife, as is done by the courts of equity in England, may appear to militate against this general principle, and to interrupt the harmony of the system, which could otherwise be framed for the solution of future questions. A close examination of that decision will, however, show that it is perfectly reconcileable.

Jacob Yohe, the plaintiff in error, was the son-in-law of the intestate, whose administrators were defendants. He was largely indebted to the estate, and an execution had issued, though without effect, on account of his insolvency. At the death of the intestate, which was subsequent to the execution, a writ of partition was issued by the orphans' court; and as the real estate was found not to be susceptible of division, it was awarded to certain of the children upon their giving sufficient security according to law, for the shares of the other heirs, of whom Yohe's wife was one. The administrators petitioned the orphan's court to order the debt of the husband to the estate of the intestate, to be deducted from the share of the wife; but without success. The circuit court, on appeal reversed the decree, and it came finally for argument before the supreme court.

The ground taken by the counsel for the appellant, was that the bond being given for real estate, ought to

* 1 Binney's Rep. 358

be considered as such; the husband could therefore have in it but a life estate, and it was the duty of the court, like a court of chancery, to secure a settlement out of the property for the wife, and to prevent its exposure to the payment of the husband's debts.*

Chief Justice Tilghman, who delivered the opinion of the court, briefly said,† that this was a call made upon them for the exertion of a chancery *power*, of which no trace could be found in our courts, and that the presumption therefore was that they did not possess it. Yohe's debt to Barnet's estate was in consequence deducted from his wife's purpart, and no settlement was insisted upon.

The interference of the court of chancery in order to enforce the equity of a party, is a matter not so much of strict right or *debitum justitiæ*, as of grace and favour. Whenever, therefore, a complainant refuses to comply with the terms which the chancellor wishes to impose upon him, the latter may refuse to assist him in his cause, or to allow him the advantage of the process of the court. A court of law on the contrary is constrained to render justice, without the power of denial or delay. The cause of this distinction may be traced to the various origins of the two jurisdictions: the chancellor succeeded to the equitable powers of the king, who alleviated the rigour of the law, as a matter of mercy; while courts of law were established in order to administer the ordi-

* 1 Binney, 360. There were other grounds taken, but this is the only one that relates to my subject.

† 1 Binney, 365.

nary rules, which were the strict right of the subject. Whenever a husband has a *legal* right to the property of his wife, he may take it to his own use without restriction, and chancery will not prevent him by injunction;* it is only when the interposition of *equity* is necessary to his obtaining possession, that he will be compelled to do *equity*. The right to declare to a party to whom property has been awarded, that he shall not take it, except upon certain conditions, is therefore a chancery power, which might perhaps be exercised by a jury, through the medium of their verdict, but which was neither vested in the court by immemorial usage, or by an act of the legislature.† The only mode in which the judiciary have felt themselves authorised to trench upon the common law, is by an administration of equity through the medium of legal forms; they have never ventured by their mere act to assume the *powers* of chancery, and to do that which the chancellor would do.‡ If the objection to the payment of the wife's share by the administrators had arisen from *their* desire, that a settlement should be made upon her, on a suit brought by the husband, they might have

* Milner-*v*-Colmer, 2 P. Wms. 641.

† It is remarkable that throughout the whole of this argument, the supreme court appears to have been regarded as sitting in its ordinary capacity as a court of law; it does not seem to have been considered, that while passing upon an appeal from the orphan's court, which is a court of chancery within the extent of its jurisdiction, it possessed of course the same powers. At least this ground was not urged in the argument.

‡ Dorrow-*v*-Kelly, 1 Dall. 144.

pleaded this equitable defence, either generally or specially, and it is probable that the court would have held it sufficient; because it was an equity enforced in chancery, and was brought before them regularly through the medium of the forms of the common law.*

Thus it appears that in order to reduce the rule of Yohe-*v*-Barnet to an uniformity with the principles laid down in other cases, it was only necessary to turn a strict and undivided attention to the obvious difference between the principles and powers of equity. The general rule is therefore clearly established, that a Pennsylvania court of law is at the same time a limited court of equity, and will administer justice according to the principles of the latter, so far as it can be done through the medium of the forms of the common law. By applying this principle to every case which may hereafter occur, a complete and easy solution is attainable.

When we consider the difficulties which the forms of the common law opposed to the introduction of equity,

* Rees Moore et al.-*v*-Owen Jones et al. Common Pleas of Philadelphia county, December term, 1804, No. 229. This was an action brought under the insolvent laws of Pennsylvania, by the trustees of the effects of a debtor, against the executors of his wife's father, for a legacy left to her a short time before her husband's insolvency. The parties referred all matters in variance between them, to Messrs. Jared Ingersoll, Peter S. Du Ponceau, and James Gibson. These gentlemen proceeding upon the principle that equity was a part of the law of Pennsylvania, awarded to the wife, by their report filed, what they deemed a proper portion out of the property left to her, for the maintenance of herself and her children.

and the shortness of the period which has produced this beneficial revolution, it is surprising that it should yet have progressed so far as to be capable of reduction to a point, bearing even a distant resemblance to order or system. It is only since the year 1787, when the case of Pollard-*v*-Shafer was decided, that equity has begun to attract serious attention as a part of the jurisprudence of Pennsylvania: the faint glimmerings which may be discovered in cases of an earlier date, shed but a feeble light upon a subject which required frequency of decision and close investigation. Yet how imperfect was the idea entertained of the principles of equity, and the modes by which chancery proceeds, even by the eminent judge who delivered the opinion in Pollard-*v*-Shafer, and how inferior to the system, which under the fostering care of the courts is now gradually progressing. The difference between courts of law and equity he describes to be, that the first is bound by strict rules, while the latter "judges of every case according to the peculiar circumstances attending it, and is bound not to suffer an act of injustice to prevail."* This is a description of equity as it was in its infancy; at the present day its rules are as fixed and certain as the rules of law, and are adhered to as inflexibly.† A decided point is never discussed; and the discretion of the chancellor, far from being a mere arbitrary will, deciding each case upon its own peculiar footing, and

* 1 Dall. 212.

† Bond-*v*-Hopkins, 1 Sch. & Lefr. 428-9.—Fry-*v*-Porter, 1 Mod. Rep. 307.

always recurring to first principles, is a sound discretion, governed by rule, permanent and regular.

The equity which the courts are now establishing in Pennsylvania, is founded upon just notions, both of the rules of chancery, and that which is expedient for the public benefit. In its administration the judges consider themselves and the jury as much bound by the principles of equity as by the positive precepts of law; and the respective provinces of the two component branches of the judicial power, are separate and well defined. The facts which require the interposition of equity must be ascertained by the jury; but the extent, the species, and the manner of the relief, are considered as pure questions of law, and therefore, the proper province of the court.* In this manner the system is orderly and well regulated, and is rendered less liable to inconvenience.

If Pennsylvanian equity had obeyed the impulse given to it, by the case of Pollard-*v*-Shafer, it would vary with the change of juries; there could be no certainty in advice, no security in action. Every case would depend upon the impression it could make upon the minds of the jurors, which is too frequently accidental, and as changeful as the characters and dispositions of men. As it is, the want of a court of chancery, which would otherwise be insupportable, has been in a great measure supplied, more certain and ample justice is done in

* Witman-*v*-Ely, 4 Serg. & R. 266.—Jones-*v*-Maffet, 5 Serg. & R. 528-9.—Griffith-*v*-Chew, 8 Serg. & R. 26.—Peebles-*v*-Reading, 8 Serg. & R. 491.

every case to the suitor, and the mixed stream of law and equity flows in one even and undisturbed current.

THE CHANCERY POWERS POSSESSED BY THE COURTS OF PENNSYLVANIA.

In the administration of equity, as we have seen from an examination of the case of Yohe-*v*-Barnet, care must be taken to distinguish between its powers and principles. The practice and rules relating to the latter, could be settled by the decisions of the courts; but to introduce the former, the interference of the legislature or immemorial custom was absolutely necessary. In order to give a complete view of our equitable system, it is therefore necessary to enumerate the provisions of the various acts which have conferred chancery powers upon the courts. The distinction between this and the former branch of my subject, is that in the one the forms of the common law are indirectly the vehicles of equity; while in the other, application is immediately made to its original conductors, the powers of chancery.

The sixth section of the fifth article of the constitution of the state, is that which regulates the chancery powers of the courts, and forms therefore the natural point of commencement for an examination of this subject. It is there provided, that in addition to the powers before exercised by them, the supreme court and the several courts of common pleas shall have the powers of a court of chancery, so far as they relate to the perpetuating of testimony, the obtaining of evidence from places not within the state, and the care of the persons and estates of those who are *non compotes mentis*. The concluding paragraph invests the legislature with an authority to grant to the courts such other equitable powers as may be found necessary; and from time to time to enlarge or diminish them, or to vest them in such other courts as they may deem necessary to the proper administration of justice.

The natural division of the equitable powers of our courts is therefore into 1st, Those that existed prior to the formation of the constitution, and which are therefore confirmed by it; and 2dly, Those that have been granted by the legislature since 1790, by virtue of the authority conferred upon them. Of the powers given by the constitution. it is unnecessary to speak; they are treated at length in the elementary books of chancery practice, and a general reference is therefore amply sufficient.*

The chancery powers possessed by the courts of common law prior to 1790, were extremely limited in their operation, and indeed almost confined to those granted by the constitution of 1776, which were afterwards introduced without alteration into the new constitution. But two other powers had been previously granted by the legislature, which may be properly classed with those of a court of equity.

I. The power exercised by the court of chancery, of supplying the loss of deeds and other writings relating to lands and tenements, from particular necessities created by the war of the revolution, became an object of primary importance. The invasion of the British

* 1 Maddock's Chan. 152.—2 Maddock's Chan. 565.

army had caused many of the inhabitants to conceal their deeds under ground; and there they had either become defaced and illegible, or from the subsequent deaths of their concealers, the clues to their discovery had been lost.* It was but justice on the part of the legislature to relieve persons so circumstanced; and an act was passed in 1786, giving to the judges of the supreme court the requisite power. The proceedings under this act are the same as in ordinary chancery cases. The application must be made by bill or petition, setting forth the facts and circumstances of the case; upon which a subpœna issues, giving notice to all persons interested in the cause to appear within a given time. If the answer be filed, or the parties subpœnaed neglect to appear, the judges must examine the witnesses produced, or cause their depositions to be taken; from which they are to make their decree, as shall appertain to justice and equity.† The record of these proceedings will be sufficient evidence of the former existence of the deed, and the party's right to its renewal. An act passed in 1793 makes the former act perpetual, and extends the same powers to the courts of common pleas.‡

II. In the year 1789,§ a chancery power of great importance in its limited sphere, was granted to the courts; it is that of applying to the conscience of the garnishee in an attachment, and compelling him by means of interrogatories to discover the goods in his possession

* Preamble to the act, 2 Sm. Laws, 375.

† 2 Smith's Laws, 376.

‡ 3 Smith's Laws, 87.

§ 2 Smith's Laws, 502.

belonging to the defendant. The attachment of the property of a foreign debtor is said by Huberus,* to be the general custom of Europe; but the proceeding in Pennsylvania is more immediately derived from the practice of the city of London;† and this particular branch is an obvious imitation of the bill of discovery, which is there usually preferred on the equity side of the mayor's court.‡ If the garnishee in Pennsylvania be guilty of any unnecessary delay in making his answer, the court will expedite the recovery against him:§ the act itself which gave this application, has also provided, that on his failure of compliance, judgment may be taken as in case of confession; and an execution may issue against the property of the defaulter himself, for the whole sum claimed by the plaintiff. When the possession of sufficient property to satisfy the debt is confessed by the garnishee, judgment will be granted on motion.||

The answer of the garnishee, either totally denying that he has goods belonging to the defendant, or confessing the possession of property, insufficient to liquidate the whole demand, is by no means conclusive upon the plaintiff. He may avail himself of a trial by jury, though if he fail in proving the falsehood of the answer, he renders himself liable to the payment of costs.¶ If

* 2 Bro. Civ. and Adm. Law, 333.

† Cramond-*v*-Bank of United States, 4 S. & R. 147.

‡ Sergeant on Attachment, 23.

§ 4 Sergeant & Rawle, 147.

|| Walker-*v*-Gibbs, 2 Dall. 211.

¶ Walker-*v*-Wallace, 2 Dall. 113.—Walker-*v*-Gibbs, 2 Dall. 211.

the verdict be against the garnishee, the jury must find specifically the goods in his possession; and execution will issue for them, or for the value set upon them in the verdict,*

As these are the only chancery powers granted by the legislature of Pennsylvania to the common law courts, anterior to the formation of the constitution, I will proceed at once to the enumeration of those that have been since conferred by virtue of the power there delegated.

I. If articles of agreement be made for the sale of lands, and the vendee has fulfilled his part of the contract, the vendor becomes in equity a mere trustee, and may at any time be proceeded against in England, by bill, and in Pennsylvania by action of ejectment. But if the vendor die without delivering possession, or executing the proper conveyances, the condition of the parties is in some degree changed, and there would be difficulties in the way of the attainment of justice, unless provision were made for this and similar cases. In England, when a trust has once clearly and honestly arisen, it is the duty of the court of chancery to provide against its failure, merely through the want of a trustee; and one will be appointed whenever there is a defect of this nature.† In Pennsylvania, as we have no court of chancery, this power could only be vested by acts of assembly. The legislature have been extremely careful to supply the deficiency; and most of the acts made since

* Crawford-*v*-Barry, 1 Bin. 485.

† Dunscomb-*v*-Dunscomb.—Lee-*v*-Randolph, 2 Hen. & Munf. 11, 12.—Ellison-*v*-Ellison, 6 Ves. jr. 663.

1790, to increase the chancery powers of the courts, may be reduced to this head.

In 1792, two years after the adoption of the constitution, an act was passed enabling executors and administrators to convey lands, for the sale of which their decedents had already by *writing* contracted:* the requisition of a written contract was made in consequence of our act of frauds and perjuries. In 1818, the chancery construction of the English statute was legislatively adopted; so that now, if a parol agreement for land be in part fulfilled during the life of the decedent, his representatives may complete the conveyance.† This power may also be exercised by the executor of an executor, or the administrator of goods not yet administered.‡

It is still a question at common law whether, if a testator direct that "*his executors shall sell his land,*" the right to sell will continue in the survivor; inasmuch as it is a bare power, uncoupled with an interest:§ but if the devise had been of "*the land to be sold by the executors,*" it would have admitted of no doubt, as the interest was held to pass by the first words of the clause, and not to be counteracted by the latter.‖ So refined a subtlety, which could not present itself to the minds of ordinary testators, and which, perhaps, professional

* 3 Smith's Laws, 66.

† Pamphlet Laws, 183.

‡ Act of 1804. 4 Sm. 158.

§ Harg. Co. Litt. Note 2, 113, a.

‖ Co. Litt. 181. b and 236, a.

men would sometimes overlook, could not be a favourite in a court of equity, and accordingly many cases may be found in the chancery reports, in which the execution of such a power was directed, though held extinct at law, and even though the applicants did not come under the favoured denominations of wives, children, or creditors.* Two acts of assembly, the one bearing date in 1792,† and the other in 1800,‡ have set this question (if it could have been one in Pennsylvania,§) completely at rest; so that now unless the testator has otherwise specially directed, the naked power will survive, and the trust may be executed by the living executor. If some of the executors renounce, the power will go to those who accept—if all renounce, or if they are dismissed, then to the administrator *cum testamento annexo*, or *de bonis*, as the case may be.

If an administrator, who has contracted for the sale of the decedent's lands, under an order of the orphan's court, die before the execution of the proper conveyances, the administrator *de bonis non* may supply the defect; and if no new administrator be appointed, the court will, on petition, direct the sheriff to execute the deeds, and thus complete the performance of the trust. The title will be as good and effectual at law as if originally made by the administrator.‖

* Locton-*v*-Locton, 2 Freem. 136.—Tenant-*v*-Browne, 1 Cha. Cas. 180.

† 3 Smith's Laws, 67.

‡ 3 Smith's Laws, 433.

§ Zeback-*v* Smith, 3 Bin. 72.

‖ 3 Smith's Laws, 500.

If a lunatic, when *compos mentis*, contract for the sale of his lands, his committee are by the act of 1794, appointed trustees to perfect the agreement.* The rule of the civil law, "neque testamentum rectè factum, neque ullum aliud negotium, rectè gestum, posteà furor interveniens perimit,"† had long before been adopted by the court of chancery; and as it was contrary to equity that the change in the condition of the vendor, by the act of God, should affect a trust which had honestly arisen, it was the constant practice to relieve the vendee.‡ The constitution had already vested in our courts, chancery powers, so far as they relate to the care of the estates and persons of idéots and lunatics; and it is therefore questionable whether this act is not to be considered as merely declaratory of an existing power.

One general remark may be made upon all these acts, that they are merely enabling, not compulsive. The executors and administrators of decedents, and the committees of lunatics, might if they pleased, when the contracts of their several principals were proved, according to the chancery method pointed out by the act of 1794,§ refuse to perform the agreement specifically, and thus compel the vendees to have recourse to the action of ejectment, upon their equitable rights, or to the taking of conditional damages, in an action on the

* 3 Smith's Laws, 129.

† Inst. lib. 2, tit. 12. s 1.

‡ Owen-*v*-Davis, 1 Vez. 82.

§ 3 Smith's Laws, 66.

case, for the failure of the performance. This difficulty was in a great measure provided against by an extremely beneficial act, passed at a late session of the legislature,* which gives a more direct and immediate remedy.

The first section invests the supreme court, in general terms, with *all* the powers of a court of equity so far as they regard the appointment of trustees, to supply the places of those who in consequence of death, infancy, lunacy, or other disability, are incapable of performing the trusts committed to them; or who refuse to act under the appointment of the *will* or *deed.* At the death of one of co-trustees, who are to perform a joint act, the court are empowered to appoint another in his place, and may compel the re-conveyance of the legal estate, where the trust has expired.

The mode of proceeding in order to obtain the advantages granted by this act, is pointed out by the second section, and bears a strong resemblance to the chancery practice. A petition in the manner of a bill in equity is to be presented by the *cestuy que trust,* or other person interested, in which, under oath or affirmation, he is to set forth the facts of his case. The court, without the intervention of a jury, will then hear and determine the matters contained in it; and on sufficient cause shown, will supersede the former trustees, and vest their powers in others as completely as if they

* Act of 22d March, 1825, Pamphlet Laws, 107. It was probably intended by this act, to comprehend all cases of failure of trusts; but a deficiency has lately been discovered in practice. There is no provision where a trustee has in part performed his trust, but refuses to complete it.

had been originally appointed in the will or deed, and as fully as a court of equity might do.

The third section provides that on fulfilment of their trusts, trustees may file their accounts in the supreme or district court, or in the several courts of common pleas, and exhibit a statement of receipts and expenditures, on oath. A citation will then issue, requiring the parties interested to appear; and on hearing, the court will discharge the trustees, or otherwise, as may appear to them just and equitable.

In all trusts arising from *wills* or *deeds*, the equitable provision is therefore complete: and it is only in those which arise from the *agreement* of the parties without deed, that the chancery *powers* of our courts fall short of those exercised in England.

II. A court of chancery can compel a party to produce such papers in his possession as may be of importance, in order to form a fair and accurate judgment of the point at issue. By an act bearing date in 1798,* intended to remedy the failure of the means of doing justice, occasioned by the want of this equity power, the supreme court and the several courts of common pleas are empowered, on motion and sufficient cause shown by affirmation or affidavit, and proper notice given, to require the production of such books and writings as are pertinent to the case. If the party refuse to produce them, or to satisfy the court that it is not within his power, judgment must be given as in cases of non-suit or default, as far as relates to such parts of the demand

* 3 Smith's Laws, 303.

or defence to which the books and papers are alleged to apply.

It is to be regretted, that although this law was enacted with a liberal view, and in order to supply in some measure the chancery bill of discovery, yet the courts of Pennsylvania have considered themselves bound to construe it, strictly, on account of its being "*highly penal.*" The rule was so laid down in Rose-*v*-King;* and will govern all cases arising under the act of assembly.

III. The third chancery power granted to the courts of common law, since the year 1790, enables the committees of *non compotes*, to sell lands where this power did not before exist.

In the article of the constitution which gives to the courts the custody of lunatics, as exercised in England by the court of chancery, there is an error, slight indeed, but singular, when the legal knowledge of its principal framers is taken into consideration. The court of chancery has no jurisdiction over cases of lunacy: the power is usually delegated to the chancellor by a special commission, and is personal, not official.† It is entirely a matter of discretion with the king, that the wardship of

* 5 Sergeant and Rawle, 244. This statute is rarely resorted to in practice. It is supplied by a notice to produce papers at the trial of the cause, without affidavit or an order of court. If the papers are not produced, copies may then be given in evidence, or the contents otherwise proved; and the refusal of the party is left to work upon the jury to his prejudice.

† 2 Maddock's Chancery, 566.—2 Fonblanque's Equity, 224.

non compotes should be granted to him;* and one instance has occurred in which it was conferred upon the lord treasurer.†

Considered then as the king's special commissioner, and representing him, in his capacity of *parens patriæ*, the chancellor with the advice and assistance of the next of kin and the heir, may do whatever is for the lunatic's advantage; such as cutting timber, or selling the real estate for the payment of debts.‡ The committee may with the permission of the court, mortgage the estate in order to raise money for necessary purposes.§ But in all these instances the advantage must be immediately to the lunatic or his estate, and I can find no case which authorises a sale for the benefit, or even common maintenance of his family. This was a defect in the law, and has therefore been supplied by the legislature.

By an act bearing date in 1814, the real estates of persons *non compotes* may be sold, on application of their committees to the court of common pleas, for the payment of debts, and for the maintenance and support of themselves and their families.‖ By the act of 1818, power is given to mortgage the lands in the same manner and for the same purposes. ¶

IV. The power with which I propose to conclude

* Ex parte Phillips, 19 Ves. jr. 121.

† 2 Dick. 553.

‡ Ex parte Phillips, 19 Ves. jr. 122.

§ Foster-*v*-Merchant, 1 Vern. 262.

‖ Pamphlet Laws, 45.

¶ Pamphlet Laws, 301.

this enumeration of the chancery powers of our courts of common law, should not, perhaps, in strictness be ranked with them, inasmuch as it is not exercised in England: but as it is an authority of an extraordinary nature, and nearly akin to those of a court of chancery relating to infants and *non compotes*, it would be improper to omit it, in a dissertation upon the subject of equity in Pennsylvania.*

Every one who is not a minor, a lunatic, or an ideot. is allowed at common law to manage his own estate without restriction, and with perfect freedom from the prohibitions of the civilians in relation to prodigality. "Sic utere tuo, ut alienum non lædas," is said to be the only regulation of domestic economy, prescribed by the law of England:† yet this is scarcely a reason for the permission of wastefulness, as the acts of a prodigal are an immediate injury to his family, who have a powerful right by the law of nature, to a proper maintenance and support.‡ The law of Pennsylvania steers a middle course between the two systems. At the same time that it acknowledges like that of England, and anxiously guards the right of its citizens to the use of their property, it restricts one, and by far the most dangerous species of prodigality.

An *habitual drunkard* is as incapable of managing his affairs as an ideot or a lunatic; and yet the common law

* In New York this affinity has been perceived, and the power is therefore vested in the chancellor.

† 1 Fonblanque's Equity, 66.—1 Blackstone's Comm. 306.

‡ 1 Rutherforth, 160.

would enforce his contracts against him, as he was held to be voluntarily mad, and therefore unworthy of protection.* Equity would however in some cases relieve; more especially when the intoxication of the party arose from the fraud and contrivance of his adversary.†

The mode of proceeding in Pennsylvania in order to disable habitual drunkards from injuring themselves and their families, by improvident dispositions of their estates, is nearly the same as that pointed out by the civil law in relation to prodigals generally. "Solent prætores si talem hominem invenerint, qui neque tempus, neque finem expensarum habet, sed bona sua, dilacerando et dissipando profundit, curatorem ei dare, exemplo furiosi; et tamdiu erunt ambo in curatione, quamdiu, vel furiosus sanitatem, vel ille bonos mores receperit."‡ So in Pennsylvania, on application by petition, of any relation by blood or marriage, except the wife or a child, to the court of common pleas, commissioners will be appointed to inquire into the facts, as in cases of lunacy. If they find the charge to be true, two persons who shall be neither the heirs or the next of kin to the drunkard, shall be appointed to manage his estate, and to take care of his person until proof is given of his complete reform. No contracts made by him, between the finding of the inquisition and its discharge, will be binding either upon his real or personal estate.§

By an act subsequent to that in which these provi-

* Co. Litt. 247.—Plowd. Comm. 19.

† Johnson-*v*-Mendicott, 3 P. Wms. 130.

‡ ff. 27, 10, 1.

§ Act of 1819. Pamphlet, 75.

sions were made, the trustees may, on application to the court for permission, sell or mortgage the real estate of the drunkard for the payment of his debts, and the maintenance of himself and his family.*

In a country so constituted as this, such regulations were essentially necessary: and experience, the true test of the excellence of all laws, has shown them to be eminently beneficial. Instances have already occurred in which, by the deprivation of the means of licentiousness in the manner prescribed by the law, the offender has been completely reformed: and where this has not happened, his estates have been preserved from the otherwise inevitable consequence of his vices.

THE ORPHANS' COURT.

Having thus concluded the list of chancery powers, exercised by the courts of *common law*, it is necessary, in order to give a complete view of equity in Pennsylvania, that I should venture upon a brief outline of the jurisdiction of the orphans' court. So far as its limited authority extends, this court is a complete court of equity, proceeding according to the forms of chancery, in a great degree simplified, and invested with the same powers, to enforce its sentences and decrees. As its cognisance is limited, and whatever has not been granted to it, either expressly or by strong implication, is held to be denied,† a

* Act of 1822. Pamphlet, 4.

† Ex parte Pleasants.—Gordon's L. of Dec. 28.—1 Journal of Jurisprudence, 316.

special enumeration of its various powers is absolutely necessary.

The jurisdiction of the orphans' court is a mixture of parts of those of the spiritual and equitable courts of England, with new regulations and powers arising from our own peculiar necessities and the change of circumstances. Like the first it will revoke letters of administration which have been irregularly or improperly granted;* it will compel the distribution of the personal estate,† and in some cases will appoint administrators:‡ like the second it exercises the parental authority of the nation, over the persons and estates of those who are incapable by reason of infancy, of a proper and discreet management: and as estates are here partible, it will cause a partition to be made on application of the widow, children, or their guardians.§ To examine minutely the various branches of this important jurisdiction, would of itself require a copious and extensive commentary. I will therefore regard only those points in which it has succeeded to, and supplied the powers of the court of chancery, all of which may be classed under the following heads.

* Act of 1713, Sec. 2. 1 Smith's Laws, 82.—2 Burn's Ecclesiast. Law, tit. Wills. 643.

† Act of 1794, Sec. 1. 3 Sm. Laws, 144.—2 Burn's Ecclesiast. Law, tit. Wills. 704.

‡ Gordon's Law of Decedents, 90.—Orphans' Legacy, 71.

§ Act of 1794, Sec. 22. 3 Sm. Laws, 151. The jurisdiction exercised by the court of chancery in relation to partitions, extends to joint-tenants, tenants in common, and co-parceners. It is therefore essentially different from that of the orphans' court.

I. The controul over the persons and estates of minors.

II. The power of awarding to a widow her distributive share of an intestate's estate.

III. That of enforcing the warrants and decrees of the court.

I. The protection of the weak from the aggressions of the strong, by the united force of the community, is one of the advantages of civil society, for which, at its original formation, our natural liberty was bartered. In every government there is, therefore, a power lodged somewhere for the protection of infants, who by accident or misfortune have been deprived of their natural guardians. This tutelage was one of the branches of the authority of the Roman Prætor;* and in England it is vested in the king, as a part of his prerogative, and was exercised by his deputy, the chancellor, until the establishment of the court of wards and liveries, by Henry VIII.† At the dissolution of that mischievous and tyrannical jurisdiction it returned to its ancient channel.‡ In Pennsylvania some of these powers, possessed by the chancellor, were at a very early period of our history delegated to the orphans' court,§ and have been exercised by it until the present day.

The best mode of considering this jurisdiction, will be by a brief sketch, under the following heads.

* L. 1. ff. de minor.

† Lord Falkland-*v*-Bertie, 2 Vern. 342.—2 Fonblanque's Equity, 224.

‡ Smith-*v*-Smith, 3 Atk. 304.

§ Penn's Letter to the Society of Free Traders, 1 Proud's History, 262.

1st, Those which relate to the advancement of the personal interest of the minor.

2d, Those which are preventive; and

3d, Those which are remedial of injuries to his estate.

1st. When minors are under the age of fourteen, which by the rules of the common law, entitles them to the choice of guardians, the orphans' court will appoint proper persons to be their guardians, next friends, or tutors,* as these officers are absolutely necessary to the welfare and interest of the minor. In the creation and exercise of this power the legislature of Pennsylvania has rejected the barbarous suspicions of the common law,† and the ward may be committed to the heir, without regard to the tender fears of Glanville and Coke, that this was "quasi agnum lupo committere ad devorandum."‡ The only restrictions placed upon the discretion of the orphans' court, are that the guardian should be of the same religious persuasion that was professed by the parents of the minor, of good repute, and in accordance with the inclination of the latter, so far as he has discretion to express it.§ The court of chancery in its exercise of the same power is not absolutely governed by the same restrictions: it will not interfere in order to cause the education of children in a particular religion, unless the intention of the father be clearly expressed in his will:|| and as to the second requisite in

* Act of 1713, Sec. 7. 1 Smith's Laws, 84.

† Graham's Appeal, 1 Dall. 136.

‡ Co. Litt. 88, b.

§ Act of 1713, Sec. 12. 1 Sm. L. 85.

|| Storke-*v*-Storke, 3 P. Wms. 52.

Pennsylvania, the choice of the infant, though in general a proper regard is paid to it, yet the selection is held liable to reasonable objections, and the court will in every case exercise its discretion.*

The binding of minors as apprentices to trades, husbandry, and other employments, at the instance of executors, administrators, guardians or tutors,† is another power of the orphans' court, conferred for the advancement of the personal interest of the infant. Notwithstanding its general superintendance of the concerns of minors, the court of chancery has never exercised a power of this nature; of which perhaps the reason is, that no minor becomes a ward of court until he has at least filed a bill in it;‡ and persons of the inferior ranks in life rarely have occasion to make such an application. In this case, as in the appointment of guardians, the orphans' court must regard the religious persuasion of the person to whom the infant is to be bound, as well as his private inclination.§

When the personal estate is insufficient for the maintenance and education of the infant, and for the improvement of the realty, the guardian‖ or administrator¶ will be permitted, under the direction of the orphans' court, to sell so much of the real estate as is necessary, in order to effect these purposes. The court of chancery, which

* Nicoll's case, 2 Vez. 375.

† Act of 1713, Sec. 7. 1 Sm. Laws, 84.

‡ Butler-*v*-Freeman, Ambler, 303.

§ Act of 1713, Sec. 12. 1 Sm. L. 85.

‖ Act of 1807, Sec. 10. 4 Sm. L. 401.

¶ Act of 1705, Sec. 6. 3 Sm. L. 157.

in England possesses the same power, exercises it with jealousy, and only in extreme cases;* indeed it very rarely occurs that it will allow even a personal capital to be invaded.† In Pennsylvania, provided by the settlement of the administrator's account, it plainly appears that the personalty is inadequate, an order for the sale of the whole or a part of the realty, according to the act of assembly, must be made of course.‡

The last instance in which the court can interfere for the personal advantage of the minor, is to direct the placing at interest of his personal property by executors, administrators, guardians, and trustees.§ If the transaction be made *bona fide,* and the security taken with the approbation of the court, a subsequent loss will fall, as it is equitable that it should, upon the estate of the minor.‖ The principle adopted by our courts from the court of chancery,¶ is that the guardian has a right to

* Inwood-*v*-Twyne, Ambler, 419-20.

† Walker-*v*-Wetherall, 6 Ves. jr. 474.

‡ In the civil law there is a provision of the same nature, pro hibiting the alienation of the real estate, and even of the goods of a minor to a large amount, without the decree of a magistrate. D. 27, 9, 1.

§ Act of 1713, Sec. 4. 1 Sm. L. 83.

‖ Ibidem.

¶ Littlehales-*v*-Gascoyne, 2 Bro. 73. The court of chancery has evidently borrowed this principle from the civil law. "Si post depositionem pecuniæ, comparare prædia tutores neglexerunt, incipient in usuras conveniri; quanquam enim a prætore, cogi eos oportet ad comparandum, tamen si cessent, etiam usuris plectendi sunt, tarditatis gratia, nisi per eos factum non est quominus compararint." L. 7. § 3 ff. de adm. et per tut.

preserve a reasonable fund for the defraying of contingent expenses; but that if he use the surplus of the personal estate, or might, but for his negligence or fraud, have placed it out advantageously, he makes himself liable for interest.*

2d. In order to *prevent* the injuries which might possibly ensue to the estates of minors from the infidelity of their guardians, the court in their discretion may require a bond with sufficient security, even though they were selected by the testaments of parents or the choice of the minors.† Every guardian must render an account at least once in three years, and oftener if required; on sufficient cause shown, the court may remove him from his office, order a faithful delivery of all the minor's property, and make any other decree required by the interests of the latter.‡

If the register grant letters of administration without taking a bond with sureties, for the faithful performance of the duty, he becomes liable in his own proper estate for all the damages that accrue in consequence of his neglect; and the administrator is subject to the burthens of an executor *de son tort.*§ If there be sureties given, who, however, prove insufficient, the court will compel the giving of others, with such penalties as they may in their discretion judge proper: and if it appear that the administrators have wasted or misapplied any part of the

* Fox-*v*-Wilcocks, 1 Bin. 199.—Say's Executors-*v*-Barnes. 4 S. & R. 116.—Baker-*v*-Davis, 8 S. & R. 16.

† Act of 1821, Sec. 1. Pamphlet, 153.

‡ Ibidem, Sec. 3. 154.

§ Act of 1713, Sec. 2. 1 Sm. Laws, 82.

estate, or if they refuse to give the bonds demanded of them, the letters of administration will be revoked, and may be granted again to any other person entitled by law to receive them, who will comply with the demands of the court.*

There is a similar provision in the civil law, by which the interest of the infant is even more jealously guarded. The inferior magistrate who granted the guardianship, is liable not only where he has entirely neglected to take security, (the only responsibility of our *register*) but even when those sureties have proved partially or wholly insufficient.†

When a complaint is made to the court that an executrix having minors of her own, or being concerned for others, has re-married or is about to be re-married, without securing their portions or estates, it will compel her to give security for the faithful performance of the trust, and the maintenance and education of the children.‡ The same precaution will be observed in the case of an executor or other person entrusted with the estates of minors, who is like to prove insolvent, or who neglects to give a faithful inventory or account of the property which has come into his hands or knowledge.§

The last instance in which the court will interfere for

* Act of 1713, Sec. 2. 1 Sm. Laws, 82.

† L. 4. C. de Magistr. Conv.

‡ Act of 1713, Sec. 3. 1 Sm. L. 83. The civil law has provided for a like case, by making the estate of the husband a pledge for the fidelity of the wife, and the security of the minor. C. 8. 15. 6.

§ Act of 1713, Sec. 3. 1 Sm. L. 83.

the prevention of injuries to the estates of minors, is when a sale of lands has been decreed for their maintenance and support.* Before the guardian can proceed to the execution of the requisite conveyances, he will be compelled to give security for the proper disposition of the purchase money, and the investment of such parts of it as are not immediately necessary for the fulfilment of the ends of the sale.

3d. The remedial power of the court may be called into action when the injury to the estate of the minor has been already committed, so that it is too late to interfere by way of prevention. According to the civil law the guardian might be compelled by the prætor to render an exact account of his proceedings, and to exhibit an inventory of the property, whenever circumstances occurred which rendered it necessary.† In England, the minor by his prochein amy,‡ and even a stranger,§ may call the guardian to account in the court of chancery. The powers of our orphans' courts, in this respect are extremely ample, and provide a very effectual remedy. They may compel the appearance of guardians, trustees, tutors, executors, administrators, and all other persons who have been entrusted with, or are accountable for the real or personal estate of the infant; and may enforce the exhibition by them of true inventories and accounts of the estate, and the production by the register or his deputies of true copies of all pro-

* Act of 7th April, 1807, Sec. 10. 4 Sm. L. 401.

† L. 5. § 11. ff. de reb. eor. qui sub tut. 2 Fonbl. 250.

‡ Lord Falkland-*v*-Bertie, 2 Vern. 342.

§ Earl of Pomfret-*v*-Lord Windsor, 2 Vez. 484.

ceedings whatsoever in his office. If it appear to the judges that a person coming under any one of these general denominations, has misbehaved to the injury of the minor, they are required to make a certificate of it, which will be good evidence to entitle the party grieved to recover at law.* Against an administrator the remedy under an old act of assembly† is more simple and expeditious; the orphans' court, after having heard his defence, may compel him to pay over the amount found due to a minor, without the tedious and dilatory process of a suit at common law.‡

A guardian who misbehaves, or fails in the performance of the duties of his office, as by not rendering an account of his transactions, may be removed by order of the orphans' court, and compelled by its sentence to assign to his successor every thing in his possession appertaining to the infant.§

II. The jurisdiction exercised by the court of chancery in cases of dower, was assumed on account of the difficulties that attended the recovery of the widow at law, and not from any want of liberality in the ordinary courts. As the heir was possessed of the deeds, by which her claim was to be ascertained and supported against him, his conscience was affected by the concealment, and the chancery application was therefore considered the most proper and effectual remedy. Still,

* Act of 1713, Sec. 1. 1 Sm. L. 82.

† Act of 1705, Sec. 1. 3 Sm. L. 156, confirmed by the act of 1794, Sec. 1. 3 Sm. L. 144.

‡ Richards' Case, 6 Serg. & R. 464.

§ Act of March 30th, 1821, Sec. 3. Pamph. 154.

however, the claim of dower is a mere legal demand; and where the right of the widow is disputed in equity, she will be sent to establish it at law.*

The power delegated to the orphans' court by the legislature of Pennsylvania, applies only where the husband is dead intestate, and the widow claims her distributive share; it is, therefore, as to the cases embraced by its operation, more limited than that of the court of chancery. The mode of calling it into action is by petition of the widow for an order to make partition. The court will then appoint for that purpose seven or more persons on behalf and with the consent of the parties, or if the parties cannot agree in the selection, an inquest will be awarded. On a return made, a judgment will be given, that the partition shall remain firm and stable forever. A just appraisement must be made by the persons appointed by the court, if from the nature of the estate it cannot be divided without prejudice, and the widow's right shall be apportioned and charged upon the land in the possession of the child or children to whom it is awarded; if the annual interest be in arrear, it may be distrained for, as rent.† If the land be sold on account of the refusal of the heirs to take it at its appraised value,‡ the proceeds are distributable as real estate, by the personal representatives of the deceased, and the

* Curtis-*v*-Curtis, 2 Bro. Chan. Rep. 631.—1 Maddock's Chancery, 242.

† Act of 1794, Sec. 22. 3 Sm. Laws, 151.—Act of 1807, Sec. 6. 4 Sm. Laws, 400.

‡ Act of 1804. Sec. 1. 4 Sm. Laws, 184.

widow is, of course, only entitled to the interest of her share, during her life.*

When by reason of the testacy of the husband, or a forcement of the widow, the orphans' court is without jurisdiction, recourse must be had to the ancient writs of *right of dower*, and of dower *unde nihil habet*. From the prevailing liberality of our practice, these proceedings are not attended with the difficulties and delays which are supposed in England to be the necessary concomitants of a real action. Many of the ancient and unnecessary forms are omitted, and modern innovations have in some degree assimilated the practice to that of ordinary actions. It may be also proper to observe, that as conveyances are generally recorded in Pennsylvania, no widow need be ignorant of the particular lands out of which she is dowable; so that the original cause of the interference of equity is supplied.†

* Diller-*v*-Young, 2 Yeates, 261. The rights of a widow under the intestate laws of Pennsylvania, are fully treated in Gordon's Law of Decedents, p. 416.

† The distributive share of the widow under the intestate laws is to be derived only from "the remaining part of any lands, tenements, hereditaments and personal estate, not sold or disposed of by will, or otherwise limited by marriage settlement. Act of 1794, Sec. 3. 3 Sm. L. 145. If there be no lawful issue, the widow is entitled to a moiety of the estate, including the mansion house; or if the estate cannot be divided, then to one-half of the rents and profits. Sec. 4. 3 Sm. L. 146. This share is in bar of her dower at common law. Sec. 13. 3 Sm. L. 148. A devise to a wife is to be taken in bar of dower, unless the contrary be expressed; but a right of choice is reserved to her. Act of 1791, Sec. 9. 3 Sm. L. 300. And the orphans' court may cite her to make an election. Act of 1811, Sec. 1. 5 Sm. L. 258.

These are the various branches of the jurisdiction exercised in England by the court of chancery, which have been granted by the legislature to the orphans' court. All other equitable powers, not specially included in these acts, cannot be exercised by it. As a natural consequence the authority with which the chancellor is invested, by virtue of his general superintendance of the concerns of minors, to consent to their marriages, or to prohibit them by injunction,* is beyond the jurisdiction of the orphans' court. In all matters, however clearly within its power, the court considers itself bound to proceed upon the principles of equity;† and the numerous decrees that have been made since its establishment, have always been framed upon this foundation. Thus an executor who had purchased the real estate of his testator at public sale, but failed to perform his engagements, so that the property was sold a second time, has been held accountable for the larger of the

As lands in Pennsylvania are chattels for the payment of debts, the widow has no claim against creditors. 1 Dall. 484. 2 Dall. 127. 1 Yeates, 75. A wife is entitled to dower out of a trust estate. 2 Serg. & R. 556.

* 1 Maddock's Chan. 276. The jurisdiction of chancery to enjoin against the marriage of infants, is doubtless to protect rank and fortune from unequal connexions, and is not, perhaps, necessary in a republican country. The hasty marriage of minors is in some measure prevented in this state, by the act of assembly imposing a penalty of £50 on clergymen performing the service without the consent of their parents or guardians.

† Guier-*v*-Kelly, 2 Bin. 299.—M'Pherson-*v*-Cunliff, Appx No. II. xliii. Gordon's Law of Decedents.

two sums for which it was struck off.* The surplus of the purchase money of land sold by order of the orphans' court, for the payment of debts, is distributable as real estate;† and a settlement made by an infant with his guardian, a short time before his coming of age, is no bar to a subsequent settlement, according to the form prescribed by the act of assembly.‡

III. The power of the court to enforce its sentences, warrants, and orders, by imprisonment of the body, and sequestration of the lands and goods of the defendant, was granted by the act of 1713; which also provided, that this authority should be exercised and possessed as fully as by any court of equity.§ As a necessary consequence of this general provision, the practice and proceedings of the orphans' court have assimilated themselves to those of the court of chancery: the commencement of the action is by petition, and a citation of the defendant:‖ the process for compelling an appearance is grounded upon the contempt of the party, as in chancery;¶ and when accounts are complicated, a reference may be had to auditors.** If a serious difficulty arise in the ascertainment of facts, the court may probably send it (although this power has been question-

* Guier-*v*-Kelly, 2 Bin. 294.

† Diller-*v*-Young, 2 Yeates, 261.

‡ Say's Ex'rs.-*v*-Barnes, 4 S. & R. 114-15.

§ Act of 1713, Sec. 8. 1 Sm. L. 84.

‖ Gordon's Law of Dec. 21.

¶ Act of 1713, Sec. 8. 1 Sm. L. 84.

** 1 Journal of Jurisp. ex parte Pleasants, p. 319.

ed,*) to be tried at law;† the mode of proof is in general by written depositions,‡ and the sentence, whether interlocutory or final, is enforced in the same manner as that of the court of chancery.§ It is not necessary to enter into the details of this part of the subject: a reference to the English manuals of chancery practice, and to Mr. Gordon's Law of Decedents,|| is amply sufficient.

OF IMPROVEMENTS

TO THE JUDICIAL SYSTEM OF PENNSYLVANIA.

The view of equity as it exists in Pennsylvania being thus concluded, it now remains, according to the plan traced by the faculty, to proceed to an examination of the instances in which powers analogous to those of a court of chancery may be introduced with advantage. This topic would gladly have been avoided, as, from its delicacy and difficulty, a student is little fitted for its discussion: but when this duty was imposed upon us, success was at least improbable, and failures must have been anticipated. Invoking, therefore, that kind indulgence of my fellow-students, which has been already so severe-

* Ex parte Pleasants, 1 Journ. Jurisp. 314.

† Yohe-*v*-Barnet, 1 Bin. 364.—Wallace-*v*-Elder, 5 Serg. & R. 143.—Finney-*v*-Moore, 8 Serg. & R. 345.—Gordon's Law of Decedents, 35.

‡ Ex parte Pleasants, Gordon, 30.

§ Act of 1713, Sec. 8. 1 Sm. 84.

|| Gordon's Law of Decedents, Philadelphia, 1825.

ly taxed, I submit the thoughts that have occurred to me to their favourable consideration.

The acts of assembly enumerated in the course of this essay, go far to remedy our present deficiencies, and fully evince the disposition of the legislature to advance our jurisprudence as near to perfection as can be attained by mortal means and the light of experience. Upon a proper representation of our present deficiencies, there can be no doubt of their amendment.

It would seem that there is no strong existing reason for the erection of a court of chancery, or even for the granting of its general powers to the courts as now established. We have already observed that the separation of the jurisdictions of law and equity was the offspring of circumstances and is of doubtful policy: in this country, by recovering the ground the former have lost in England, by taking up the improvement of the law at the point at which they stopped, we may enjoy the honour of succeeding in an enterprise in which our ancestors failed, and of raising the common law to a pitch of perfection to which they never aspired.

Equity in Pennsylvania, though ancient in its origin, in practice is *res nova;* and an important advantage is derived from that circumstance, which the establishment of a regular and complete court of chancery would effectually destroy. The great benefit of equity arises from its introducing improvements upon the ordinary law: but these have long ceased in the court of chancery, and the corrective principle is now as stationary and as fettered by ancient rules as the system it was intended to supply. There are many instances also in which the chancellor would gladly relax the rigour of former decisions, but for the uncertainty that would arise from the change of a settled regulation. All these are difficulties that need not be felt under the present administration of equity: its very irregularity authorises our judges to perfect the common law, by improving upon that which is already an improvement, and rejecting those particular principles which courts of equity would reject, if they could now disengage themselves from their own inveterate precedents.*

If we examine closely the jurisdiction of chancery, and compare the justice there administered with that which is offered by the common law, we find the exclusive advantages of the former narrowed down at the present day to diminutive dimensions, and indeed restricted to the slender superiority, which in some cases it derives from the nature of its process. The liberality evinced within a century by the eminent lawyers who have presided in the courts of common law, has

* Some remarkable instances of the operation of this advantage are already to be found in our reports. A wife cannot, in England, be endowed of a trust estate, though a husband is entitled to his *curtesy*. For this distinction no reason could be given, and its impropriety was universally acknowledged: yet chancellor after chancellor submitted to the rule, merely because it had been so decided. 1 Cruise Dig. 496. Att'y Gen.-*v*-Scott, Forrest, 138. In Pennsylvania the courts have settled this point upon the basis of reason and justice. Shoemaker-*v*-Walker, 2 S. & R. 556. In Kauffelt-*v*-Bower, 7 Serg. & R. 74. a rule of equity conferring a lien, was rejected as inapplicable to the condition of the country.

caused the legal jurisdiction to encroach gradually upon that of equity, and to recover cognisance of many cases that had before been rejected. So far, therefore, as relates to the true end of equity, the improvement of the law, experience has shown that with a proper disposition on the part of the judiciary, it may as well be attained through the medium of the ordinary forms as of the canonical process of chancery.

In addition to this malleability of the common law, and its capacity to receive new impressions from the successive exigencies of the times, it possesses adequate forms, which, with proper extension and simplification, would embrace almost every case in which there is now a necessity for the interference of equity. Many of these have fallen into unmerited and perhaps accidental neglect; though in general the intricacy of their proceedings, and the nice subtleties that attended ancient practice, were the true causes that drove the suitor into chancery. The power to compel persons to interplead, in order that a party might be safe in rendering a duty, was once an important branch of the jurisdiction of the ordinary courts, and formed a very considerable title in the law.* The writ of *audita querela* supplied not only all the cases in which chancery would interfere to prevent an improper enforcement of a judgment, but was even more extensively remedial, by granting damages where there had been a substantial injury.† The

* Danvers' Abr. tit. *Enterpleader*. Rolle's Abr. Viner's Abr. Jacobs' Law Dict. same title.

† Johnson's Digest, tit. *Audita Querela*.—Comyn's Digest, same title.

writs of right of dower and of dower *unde nihil habet*, with the exception of the now useless application to the conscience of the heir, offered a complete remedy to the widow. The compulsion of a specific performance of an agreement for the sale of land, which is now attained in Pennsylvania by an action of ejectment, was effected at common law by an action of covenant.* The action of account render purges the conscience of the defendant, and with some modifications called for by the liberal spirit of the age, might be made to possess every other advantage that could possibly be derived from chancery process. The ancient writ of *estrepement* could have been extended so as to supersede in many instances the necessity of an injunction. Many more examples might be cited; but these are amply sufficient to prove the truth of a general remark, that if these actions had followed those in present use in their general course of improvement, the exclusive advantages of a court of chancery, even in England, would be very inconsiderable.

No disposition is felt to assert that as these actions *now* are, they fully supply the want of a court of chancery, and that the common law needs no other assistance than that which may be derived from its own power of self-improvement. The long disuse into which these ancient forms have fallen has rendered their practice intricate, though perhaps it was once simple and convenient. To take them up at the point at which we find

* 1 Reeve's History, 477. 2 Reeve's Hist. 33. 173. 2 Wilson's Works, 276. A relic of this ancient proceeding is still to be found in the action of covenant, upon which the levying of a fine is grounded.

them, and to endeavour to simplify their proceedings by a gradual progress, would present tedious, if not insuperable difficulties: while an exertion of the legislative power would at once attain the desired result, without subjecting us to years of inconvenience.

If we admit that in some cases the common law offers no adequate relief, it does not follow that immediate recourse must be had to the forms of chancery. Though the proceedings in equity, may in particular instances be superior to those of law, yet they are far from attaining that perfection and simplicity, of which their subjects are susceptible. The proper remedy would seem, therefore, to be a re-modelling of that branch of the law which is defective, rather than the introduction of a chancery process: since the latter course would be only exchanging a greater for a less evil.

Some remarkable instances have already occurred, which exemplify the possibility and advantage of supplying the proceedings of chancery by those of the common law. In a number of cases, such as the recovery of legacies, dower, partition, &c. which in England are subject to the jurisdiction of the chancery and ecclesiastical courts, our legislature has vested the common law tribunals with power to render justice according to the ordinary forms, and the change is productive of no inconvenience in practice. A more remarkable instance of this description is to be found in the proceedings directed by an act of assembly in relation to mortgages. This branch of equity jurisdiction, so fertile in intricate questions, by a few simple regulations is reduced to an easy system. The land is placed in its true light, as merely a security for the payment of money; and on failure of performance, the right of the mortgagee is not to the possession, but merely to the liquidation of his principal and interest. The mode of proceeding is by a simple *scire facias*, upon which, if proper cause be not shown to the contrary, a judgment is entered, and execution issued.* As to the complicated questions constantly arising in chancery, in relation to notice, by a simple provision that no mortgage shall be a lien except from the date of its record, we have obviated all doubt and difficulty, and annihilated forever that endless source of litigation.† A system of legislation thus skilfully blending the equitable with the legal jurisdiction, deserves to be pursued; the more so, as it is in harmony with the course steadily followed by the judiciary from the first settlement of the colony.

By adapting the forms of the common law to the attainment of the ends of equity, important advantages are acquired without the risk of inconvenience. Our system of jurisprudence will become regular in its features, and its various branches similar in their operation. The heterogeneous qualities of the common law, the result of accident rather than design, will be amalgamated so as to form a distinct and regular whole; justice will be equally administered by an unchanging rule, and the measure of right will cease to depend upon the jurisdiction, to which the application for redress is

* Act of 1705. 1 Smith's Laws, 59.

† Act of 1820. Pamphlet Laws, 141.

made. The invaluable methods of the common law to obtain the truth of facts in dispute, by an oral examination of witnesses, and a trial by jury, will still be preserved to the party. The inadequacy of the canonical forms in this important particular, is sensibly felt in the courts of equity; and the constant practice of the chancellor to refer issues of fact, is one of the most prolific causes of delay.

Let us now proceed to exemplify this system as briefly as possible, by applying it to the most prominent objects of the jurisdiction of a court of chancery; it will then be seen that they may easily be supplied, by modes of proceeding either entirely derived from the common law, or strictly analogous in their nature.

As justice is of two kinds, *preventive* and *remedial*, the subject may be best considered under this two-fold aspect.

I. It is an opinion very frequently expressed by elementary writers, that with the exception of the writ of *estrepement*, the forms of the common law are calculated for the redress, and not for the prevention of injuries. Coke, however, in his Commentary upon Littleton, enumerates six other writs, that may be issued in order to anticipate an injury. "And note there be six writs in law that may be maintained *quia timet*, before any molestation, distresse, or impleading: as 1st, A man may have his writ of *mesne*, (whereof Littleton here speaks,) before he be distreyned. 2d, A *warrantia chartæ*, before he be impleaded. 3d, A *monstraverunt*, before any distresse or vexation. 4th, An *audita querela*, before any execution sued. 5th, A *curia claudenda*, before any default of inclosure. 6th, A *ne injustè vexes,* before any distresse or molestation. And these be called *brevia anticipantia,* writs of prevention."*

That the ancient common law offered so many writs of prevention is ample proof that its forms are capable of anticipating as well as of remedying injuries; and that the power assumed by the court of chancery might have been supplied by framing new writs to suit particular exigencies, and in some degree, by extending those already mentioned. To illustrate this possibility, it will be sufficient to examine the subject of injunctions, which are the most prominent powers of prevention exercised by the court of chancery, and therefore best suited to our present purpose.

An injunction will be issued by the chancellor in the five following cases.†

1st. To restrain the infringement of patents and copy-rights.

2d. To stay proceedings in other courts.

3d. To prevent waste.

4th. To prevent the commission of nuisances.

5th. To restrain the negotiation of bills of exchange and notes, or a transfer of stock.

1. For the first of these cases, as the power to grant patents and copy-rights is vested by the constitution in the general government,‡ and the courts of the United

* Co. Litt. 100. a.

† 1 Maddock's Chancery, 127.

‡ Constitut. U. S. A. Art. III. Sec. 2. 1.

States have all the authority of a court of chancery,* the provision is complete.

2. The right to restrain the proceedings of a court by injunction, arises from the incapacity of that court to do adequate and complete justice to a party. Thus where a suit is brought in a spiritual court, by a father for the legacy of an infant child,† or by a husband in right of his wife,‡ the proceedings will be restrained, because the lower court cannot provide for the security of the fund when recovered. As the jurisdictions of the courts of Pennsylvania are well defined, so as to prevent an improper concurrence, this restrictive power would be unnecessary; and indeed unless some material alteration were made, it would never find room for operation. The chancery power to grant injunctions against an improper enforcement of a judgment at common law, is completely supplied by the liberality with which new trials are granted, and proceedings summarily stayed or set aside on motion.§

3. At common law the only use of the writ of *estrepement* was to prevent the party against whom a judgment had been obtained, from committing waste before the delivery of possession by the sheriff.‖ By the statute of Gloucester, this power was extended to the

* Act of 1789, Sec. 11 and 13.

† Rotherham-*v*-Fanshaw, 3 Atk. 627.

‡ Meal-*v*-Meal, 1 Dick. 373. Prec. Chan. 548.

§ When the facts of which the motion is predicated, are doubtful, the court will direct an issue. Share-*v*-Becker. 8 S. & R. 242.

‖ 2 Inst. Statut. of Glouc. cap. 13. p. 328.

whole period of the pendency of the suit; and it became the practice to purchase the writ, at the same time with the original process.* By an act of our assembly,† a writ of *estrepement* will issue of course, without motion, and even in vacation, on *affidavit* presented to a judge of the supreme court, or a court of common pleas, that the defendant in ejectment is committing waste.

In order that this writ should issue, it is therefore necessary that there should be a suit pending, and waste actually committed. The court of chancery, proceeding by injunction, will give redress although there is no existing action, and the waste is only threatened;‡ for in equity no one should be compelled to wait until the injury has been completed. For the benefit of him in remainder, it will hinder the possessor of the particular estate from committing waste;§ and the reversioner will be protected against malicious destruction by the tenant, although the estate had been specially made without impeachment of waste.||

Preventive justice is for obvious reasons to be preferred to that which is merely corrective; it prevents a multiplicity of suits, and it is the only mode by which a party may be protected against a daring trespasser who has no means of repairing the wrong. But this object may be easily attained without a recurrence to the chancery proceeding. It is only necessary to extend the writ of

* 2 Inst. Statut. of Glouc. cap. 13. p. 329.

† Act of 2d April, 1803. 4 Smith's Laws, 89.

‡ Gibson-*v*-Smith, 2 Atk. 183.

§ 3 Wooddes' Lec. 400.

|| Vane-*v*-Lord Barnard, 2 Vern. 738.

estrepement still farther than was done by the statute of Gloucester, so as to embrace cases in which waste is only apprehended, and without regard to the pendency of a suit.

4. In order to call into action the power of chancery to stay the commission of a nuisance, it appears to be the modern opinion that a trial at law is necessary, of the facts of which the injured party complains.* When these are ascertained, the chancellor will either enjoin perpetually against its continuance, or if it be permanent in its nature, he may order it to be abated. During the pendency of the suit he will sometimes direct the work in dispute to be stayed.†

In addition to the action on the case, which is now the ordinary legal remedy for a nuisance, the common law offered the writs of *assize of nuisance*, and *quod permittat prosternere*. By these proceedings the plaintiff obtained judgment to abate the nuisance, and to recover damages for the injury sustained.‡ As these were real actions, they could only be maintained and defended by tenants of the freehold; and this difficulty, joined to the intricacy of their practice, caused them to fall into gradual and total disuse.

A sense of the advantages that had already been derived from the revival of ancient actions, produced in the year 1809, a trial of the assize of nuisance.§ As there

* Attorney General-*v*-Cleaver, 18 Ves. jr. 218, 220—1 Maddock's Chancery, 157.

† Ryder-*v*-Bentham, 1 Ves. 543.

‡ Baten's case, 9 Rep. 55.

§ Livezey-*v*-Gorgas, 2 Binney's Rep. 194.

was no authority to dispense with the long disused formalities and requisitions of the common law, difficulties were encountered at every step; and though the action was brought to a regular conclusion, the result was too unsatisfactory to encourage a second attempt.* There is nothing, however, in the nature of the action† that prevents its being reduced by a legislative enactment, to the simplicity of modern practice; and as chancery requires a trial at law before a decree of abatement will issue, the judgment may be equally prompt and advantageous. As to staying the nuisance *pendente lite*, it is easy to frame a writ which will attain this object, in the same manner as waste is restrained by that of *estrepement*.

5. The importance of a power to restrain the negotiation of bills of exchange and promissory notes, and the transfer of stock in dispute, may easily be perceived. If the two first come into the hands of an innocent indorsee, in the usual course of trade, the original turpitude of the transaction, or the want of consideration, is effectually cleansed; and for the convenience of commerce, no defence, however equitable, can be made by the party injured.‡

The advantage of preventing the transfer of stock in

* In Brackenridge's Law Miscellanies, p. 438, the proceedings in the case of Livezey-*v*-Gorgas are to be found at length.

† I speak here only of the assize of nuisance; the writ of *quod permittat* is in the nature of a writ of right, and therefore subject to greater delay. The assize was called by the statute of Westminster the second, *festinum remedium*. 2 Inst. cap. xxiv. 405.

‡ Chitty on Bills, 125.—Lickbarrow-*v*-Mason, 2 T. R. 70.

dispute, depends upon a different reason. It is proper that there should be a power to restrain a party whose right of possession is questioned, from defrauding the plaintiff of what may prove to be his property.

But though the fact is ascertained that these preventive powers may be introduced with advantage, it does not result that the chancery mode of proceeding by bill and answer, with all its appendages, must follow in their train. It is of little consequence whether the writ issued be called an injunction, or by any other name; but it is essential that the form of a common law process should be preserved. The writ might be framed in the nature of a *si fecerit te securum*, in order to guard against fraud and vexation; giving the defendant a right to a trial by jury, if he chose to deny the facts alleged by the plaintiff: and a discretion might be vested in the courts, to maintain or dissolve the injunction, according to circumstances. In particular cases, that admit of no doubt or dispute, a simple recognisance with sureties might be resorted to. By these means, the powers of chancery would be supplied by proceedings assimilated to those of the common law, and the unity of our system in every respect preserved.

In these five cases of injunctions, we have examples of all the methods by which the powers of equity either are or may be superseded in Pennsylvania. The first is unnecessary, from the surrender of the power to which it relates to the federal government; and the second, from the nature of our judicial establishments. The third and fourth may be supplied by an extension and simplification of actions already provided; and the last by framing new writs applicable to the circumstances of the intended relief.

II. It has been seen in the preceding pages, that the greater part of the *remedial* powers of chancery have become gradually incorporated with our own common law. 1st, By successive improvements by means of the liberal action of assumpsit for money had and received, new trials, setting aside judgments on motion, and the introduction of equitable pleadings. 2d, By the adoption of chancery principles. 3d, By various statutes providing new remedies in cases for which the common law offered no adequate relief. 4th, By the establishment of the orphans court. The narrow limits within which the exclusive advantages of chancery have been reduced by the operation of these improvements, induced the late Judge Wilson to declare that the great and indeed only view in which a separate court of equity could be deemed necessary to the judicial system of Pennsylvania, was as a commercial forum to settle disputed questions of account.* That this opinion was prematurely expressed, we can feel little hesitation in believing: since the time of that learned judge, some new and essential powers derived from those of a court of chancery have been added to our legislation; and more may yet be considered wanting, though to no very considerable extent.

There was a period when the courts of common law in England were advancing so rapidly in a system not dissimilar from the one now proposed, that the court of chancery began to entertain serious apprehensions of a

* 2 Wilson's Works, 284.

concurrence in all points, with its jurisdiction.* In their own defence, therefore, the chancellors were obliged to decide that they could not be divested of their known jurisdiction, by this unexpected change in the current of determinations at common law.† Yet the cognisance of equity is expressly founded on the inadequacy of the ordinary courts to grant relief; and it is at this day an essential averment of every bill, that there is not in the particular case, a plain, adequate, and complete remedy at the common law. This assertion has now become in effect a mere matter of form, in no manner connected with the substance of the application.

In conformity with this principle, it was provided by the 16th section of the first federal judiciary act,‡ that the equity powers of the courts of the United States should be restricted in their operation to cases in which the common law offered no adequate remedy. In the construction of this section, the courts of the United States have, however, adopted the English principles, and drawing the same line of distinction between the two jurisdictions, the common law is presumed to offer no adequate remedy wherever the court of chancery was

* When the doctrine was first broached by the courts of common law, that a *profert* might be dispensed with, Lord Hardwicke is said to have been startled. 1 Maddock's Chancery, 25. Much surprise has also been expressed by Lord Eldon. Ex parte Greenway, 6 Ves. 813. East India Company-*v*-Boddam, 9 Ves. 469.

† Atkinson-*v*-Leonard, 3 Bro. C. C. 218.—Codd-*v*-Woden, 3 Bro. C. C. 73.

‡ Act of September 24th, 1789. Sec. XVI.

in the practice of entertaining a bill.* If such a tribunal were to be established in this state, it is probable that a similar course would be followed; and the confusion into which our judicial system would be immediately thrown, can scarcely be anticipated. The acts of assembly, made to supply the want of a court of equity, would require an immediate repeal. The numerous decisions of our judges, which have liberalised and extended the operation of the common law, should be abandoned in order to make room for the new jurisdiction; and all the progress of a century, made in opposition to so many contending difficulties, would be idle and unavailing. The best result that may be anticipated is an useless concurrence, if not a dangerous collision of jurisdictions. It is easier to pursue the system which has been already so successfully begun, and now wants so little for its completion, than to retrace our steps to the point from which we started.

In the view of chancery remedies about to be taken, it will be unnecessary to enter into minute details, or to examine separately each individual branch of jurisdiction. Enough will be done to exemplify the proposed system, if the more prominent objects of equitable relief are exhibited, with the means of obtaining similar justice in the tribunals now existing, by a modified application of the ordinary forms. Subjects of minor importance will naturally follow the same course, and at a proper time, find their places in the system. The five following appear to be best deserving of present consideration.

* Robinson-*v*-Campbell, 3 Wheat. Rep. 223.

1st, Specific performance of contracts.

2d, Bill of peace.

3d, Bill to cancel deeds and other instruments.

4th, Bill for an account.

5th, Application to the conscience of the defendant.

1. We have seen in a former part of this essay, that the want of chancery powers, in relation to the specific performance of contracts, is scarcely felt in Pennsylvania, since they are *indirectly* supplied by common law proceedings, prompter in their operation, and equally beneficial in their relief. This useful object may, however, be *directly* attained by the application of a well known form of common law proceeding. The only requisites to the administration of the equitable remedy are a full proof of the agreement, and a demonstration of the complainant's right. These might be shown under a *scire facias*, calling upon the vendor to show cause why the contract should not be performed, and title deeds executed; if a sufficient defence be not exhibited, a judgment framed according to the exigency of the writ, might then be granted. This proceeding would probably be found more expeditious than an ejectment, while at the same time the equity of the case is more fully embraced, and a trial by jury preserved to the parties.

2. A bill of peace is preferred in chancery, in order to prevent a multiplicity of suits, in two cases: 1st, Where there have been repeated trials of the same right by ejectment, which have terminated against the party complained of;* and 2d, Where the right of the com-

* Leighton-*v*-Sir Edward Leighton, 1 P. Wms. 671.—S. C. 1 Strange's Rep. 404.—Lord Bath-*v*-Sherwin, Prec. in Chan. 262.

plainant may be controverted by several persons, at different times, and in distinct actions.*

The real actions anciently used to assert a title to land, were final in their nature, and concluded the right of the party. When the action of ejectment came into ordinary use, intolerable grievances would have resulted, if the court of chancery had not assumed a power to prohibit the party from proceeding at law, by a constant repetition of actions upon the same right. In the exercise of this jurisdiction, a single judgment is not held sufficient to entitle a complainant to a perpetual injunction: there must have been at least two trials at law, resulting in similar verdicts.† By preventing the evil which was the origin of the chancery power, a recurrence to its intervention has become unnecessary in Pennsylvania. An act of the legislature, passed in 1807,‡ has made two verdicts in ejectment, given in succession for either party, a bar to any future proceeding. If one verdict be given for each party, the third is conclusive. Perhaps it would be still better if ejectments were placed as to the conclusiveness of the verdict, upon the same footing with other actions; for the only ground on which this multiplicity of suits was allowed for the same cause, originated in an obsolete fiction.§

* Lord Tenham-*v*-Herbert, 2 Atk. 484.—1 Maddock's Chancery, 166.

† Robinson-*v*-Lord Byron, 2 Cox, 5, 6.

‡ Act of 1807, Sec. 4. 4 Sm. Laws, 477. And see Mitchell-*v*-Mitchell, 4 Binney's Rep. 180.

§ The plaintiff in ejectment by another demise to a fictitious person, makes a fresh action upon a supposed different right. Christian's Note, 3 Bl. Com. 205. The English common law

As to the second case in which a bill of peace may be preferred, it can be easily supplied by a writ of *scire facias,* calling upon the persons who it is supposed will controvert the plaintiff's title, to appear and show cause why it should not be confirmed, and forever quieted. When all the parties interested are thus brought into court, an issue might be framed in the same manner as in chancery, to determine the right; a judgment might then be given according to the facts ascertained by the verdict. The judgment, of course, would only be binding on those who were regularly summoned.

3. The power of the court of chancery to order the surrender of deeds, bonds, and other instruments, was anciently exercised only where at common law an action of detinue would not lie.* As in this action, the defendant has his election either to return the thing specifically, or to answer in damages, the distinction is no longer observed, and a bill may in every case be preferred.†

This proceeding in chancery strongly resembles the bill of peace in its operation, and may be supplied by the same method. All the parties concerned could be included in a *scire facias;* an issue might afterwards be directed, and a judgment entered according to the result.

courts can interfere in no other manner than by staying the proceedings until the costs of the former action are paid. 2 W. Bl. 1158.

* 9 Edw. IV. 41 B. pl. 27. In the *Registrum Brevium*, p. 159, there is the form of a writ of detinue *de chartis reddendis.* See 2 Reeve's Hist. 167.

† 1 Maddock's Chancery, 225.

In speaking of the modes by which the proceedings of chancery could be supplied, mention has been frequently made in the course of this essay of the writ of *scire facias*. No process among the forms now existing at common law, possesses so many natural advantages, and is capable of such extensive adaptation. As there is no act which a party could not be called upon to show cause why its performance should not be enjoined or prohibited, so there is, perhaps, no branch of equity jurisdiction that could not be included within its operation. Two great advantages of chancery practice are said to consist in the power to join in the action all parties concerned in the event, and the plastic nature of the decree which accommodates itself to every case, however complicated, and "equally reaches and protects the most remote and the most immediate interests."* Both of these desirable objects may be sufficiently attained by the writ of *scire facias*. The plaintiff might be allowed to make defendants of all persons whom he was desirous of concluding, and the words of the writ setting forth the relief required, would be the ground-work of the judgment. When it was intended by our legislature to supply the chancery powers relating to mortgages, the advantages of a *scire facias* were perceived, and this writ was made the instrument of the beneficial change that was operated in our system. A considerable portion of the common law jurisdiction of the chancellor, is also exercised through its intervention.†

4. The mode of supplying the extensive powers pos-

* Kauffelt-*v*-Bower, 7 Serg. & R. 78.

† Com. Dig. title Chancery, C. 1.

sessed by the court of chancery in relation to accounts, will require closer consideration, both from the intrinsic magnitude of the subject, and the importance attached to it by a learned investigator of our system.*

The disadvantages of the action of account render, the method directed by the common law for the attainment of a similar purpose, were supposed to consist in the dilatoriness of its proceedings, caused by the requisition of two judgments and the use of special pleadings before the auditors appointed to take the account. If the plaintiff succeeded in the first instance in proving that the defendant had received his property and was accountable to him, he obtained judgment *quod computet;* if the facts or law were disputed before the auditors appointed by the court, issues were formed for trial before the proper judges; and it was only after this process had been successfully pursued, under all the intricacies of the ancient forms of pleading, that the second and final judgment was obtained.

It was owing in part to these difficulties, but in a greater degree to the want in early days of the application to the conscience of the defendant, that the common law proceeding fell into disuse, and the court of chancery began to assume cognisance in matters of account. The original pretence for this interference was that the accountant was a trustee to the use of the complainant, and therefore one of the peculiar objects of equity jurisdiction.† The advantages of chancery practice over the forms then in use, soon rendered the action obsolete.

* 2 Wilson's Works, 284.

† Middleton-*v*-Dodswell, 13 Ves. 268.

The proceeding in equity by bill, is however strictly analogous to the legal method; so that wherever the party cannot recover at law, a bill will not be sustained. If the right at law be doubtful, an issue will be directed; and if it then be established, the account will be directed as a matter of course.*

As these proceedings of law and equity were concurrent with each other, there were originally but few improvements necessary in order to make the action of account as advantageous as the bill in equity. The grand obstacle, the want of power to apply to the conscience of the defendant, and to compel the production of his books and papers, was obviated by a statute of Queen Anne.† The charge of dilatoriness was the only one remaining for which a provision was necessary; and a brief comparison will show that even in this respect it could have been in no wise more culpable than the chancery proceeding.

The stages of litigation are precisely the same in the two jurisdictions, and contain similar causes of delay: if at law, you must establish your right to an account by a judgment *quod computet*, so in chancery the legal right must be proved before the account is ordered: if at law there is a reference to auditors, in order to settle the mutual claims of the parties, so in chancery there is a reference to masters: in both when facts are controverted, an issue is directed, and a final judgment is only pronounced after a report has been made. If then there

* 1 Maddock's Chancery, 86.

† 4 Anne, C. 6. S. 27.

be a difference in the expedition of suits, it must arise from some collateral circumstances, and not from a superiority of either of the modes of proceeding.

If we examine closely into the nature of the action of account, we shall find in the intricacy of its proceedings the true reason for the neglect and disuse in which it has remained. The great advantages possessed by chancery prior to the statute of Queen Anne, drew to it all litigations of this nature, at a time when practitioners were well acquainted with the mode of conducting the action; the long and total neglect into which it subsequently fell, caused much of this important learning to be forgotten, and intricacies to succeed what was probably order and regularity.

The case of Godfrey-*v*-Saunders,* which is so frequently cited as a triumphant example of what the action of account may do when properly conducted, is in truth a striking instance of the disadvantages just mentioned. The defendant was guilty of a contempt of court, in pleading to the auditors a defence tending to render nugatory the judgment *quod computet*, and upon which he had already relied before the jury. The plaintiff demurred, and upon the point that then arose, the judges felt so much hesitation that they required a second argument in order to understand it more clearly. When this had taken place they gave no directions as to the judgment to be entered, candidly confessing that they felt considerable doubt upon this point, and the mode of assessing the damages. There is reason to be-

* 3 Wilson's Reports, 95.

lieve from the record,* that the judgment upon the *demurrer* was a *nil dicit;* as the whole amount laid in the declaration was awarded by the court to the plaintiff for the value of his merchandise, together with an additional sum for his costs and damages, by reason of the *inter-pleading* and the expenses of suit. It is evident that by this random result, justice was not done to the parties: the value laid in the declaration was merely nominal, and could not properly be taken as the exact measure of damages.†

But though this case is an instance of the intricacy of the action of account render, and the difficulties presented by its complicated forms, it tends in a great measure to prove, that in point of expedition, the remedy offered by the courts of common law is equal, if not superior to the proceeding in chancery. The subject matter of the suit of Godfrey-*v*-Saunders had been depending in equity twelve years before the action was brought in the common pleas; and although objections were taken at every stage, accompanied by repeated arguments, in the space of two years it was finally concluded. The judgment was indeed loose and unsatisfactory, but little more was requisite in order to have rendered it complete.

There can be no stronger proof of the capability of the action of account render, than that notwithstanding its manifest disadvantages, it has found in learned judges admirers and defenders. Chief Justice Wilmot, after

* 3 Wilson's Reports, 94.

† The value of the goods was 9560*l.* 12*s.* 7*d.* 3 Wils. Rep. 95. The amount laid in the declaration was £12,000. Ibid. p. 74.

having called it a chaos of clashing hints, notes, and cases,* declared his satisfaction at its revival. Chancellor Kent, a still higher authority, has expressed his surprise that it should have fallen into such complete disuse.† The reference to auditors, he considers more advantageous than that to masters, and as a proof, he refers to the practice of the court of chancery and the house of lords, to appoint merchants to assist the master when the accounts are complicated. On the whole, we may therefore conclude, that when the intricacies of the action are corrected, we shall possess a remedy superior to that of a court of equity; since to the promptness of the common law, it will add the administration of equal justice, through the medium of analogous proceedings.

The legislature of Pennsylvania has evinced a disposition to cut the Gordian knot, which the judges in Godfrey-*v*-Saunders endeavoured so fruitlessly to untie. An act passed in 1821,‡ in consequence of doubts thrown out by the supreme court, in Jones-*v*-Stratton,§ has declared that the action of account render is within the compulsory arbitration act of 1810, and its various supplements,—that the arbitrators are to decide on the whole merits of the case, to report the balance due from one party to the other, and to annex to their report from the allegations and proofs of the parties, such an account as they shall think proper and just. There is, of course, no necessity while the cause is under arbitration, for

* 3 Wilson's Rep. 113-17.

† Duncan-*v*-Lyon, 3 Johns. Chan. Cas. 361.

‡ Pamphlet Laws, 152.

§ 4 Sergeant & Rawle's Reports, 76.

the preparatory judgment *quod computet;* the whole matter proceeds at once, and the action, notwithstanding the difficulties shared in common with the chancery proceeding, may sometimes be concluded with as little delay as any other mode of litigation.

There is cause to regret that when this act was under consideration, some method was not adopted to regulate appeals, and to abridge the subsequent proceedings. It is said that other sections were originally appended to it, providing that on an appeal the particular items of the account made up by the arbitrators, to which exceptions were taken, should be specified, accompanied by an oath of the appellant where the objection was to matters of fact; and that no more privity should be required between the parties, than in actions of assumpsit. Owing to some misconception of the bill, these clauses were omitted at its passage in the senate, after the whole bill had been adopted by the house of representatives. In consequence, the judges of the supreme court in a late case* felt themselves under the necessity of deciding, that upon an appeal, the action commenced *de novo*, and the various stages of proceeding should be regularly gone through. An act supplying this deficiency would tend greatly to improve the administration of justice; for it seems to be generally admitted, that the present action of account render is almost unmanageable, and would be entirely so, but for the liberality of the practitioners.

Of other improvements that yet remain to be made,

* Wright-*v*-Guy, 10 Serg. & R. 228.

the most important are, perhaps, the consolidation of issues made before auditors, so that they may be tried by the same jury; and some clear and simple regulations relating to the pleadings and judgments.

5. Whether an appeal to the conscience of a defendant, as practised in chancery, is a real advantage to a system of jurisprudence, is a question upon which serious doubts have been entertained by grave and judicious members of the profession. "How far," says Blackstone, "such a mode of compulsive examination is agreeable to the *rights of mankind*, and ought to be introduced in *any* country, may be matter of curious discussion."* This mode of proceeding is certainly opposed to the genius and spirit of the common law, and stands in marked opposition to the free character of its institutions. Considered simply as a mode of ascertaining the truth, it is liable to some striking objections. The frauds and perjuries that follow in its train, frequently defeat its very object, and throw difficulties in the way of the ascertainment of facts, from which the rules of evidence prescribed by the common law are entirely free.

It seems a questionable position, as assumed by Blackstone,† that the oath of the parties should be *universally* adopted or rejected: some particular cases may arise, affording a reasonable ground for discrimination. If in these instances, an application to the conscience should be deemed necessary, interrogatories might be administered in the same manner as to a garnishee in an attach-

* 3 Bl. Com. 381.

† Ibidem.

ment, with as slight a departure as possible from the ordinary forms of law. If it were only permitted where no other testimony can be produced, the answer of the defendant would of course be conclusive.

It is a fact not undeserving of consideration, that the bill of discovery was invented by the clerical chancellors, rather to increase their narrow jurisdiction, than from any supposed merits of that mode of investigation. The civil law, which was in general the prolific mother of chancery innovations, affords no countenance to the practice. The oath of the party is there never required to facts that are susceptible of extraneous proof; and still less could it be exacted as a matter of course. In particular cases, the *actor* or *reus*, or the prætor himself, where no other evidence was obtainable, might refer the fact in dispute to the *decisive* oath of the party, who was then obliged either to comply with the requisition, or to make a similar offer to his adversary. Unless a positive demand was made, and allowed by the judge, the oath of the party was considered voluntary and unavailing.*

When the bill of discovery was adopted by the court of chancery, it was possibly in some degree necessary, from the excessive rigour of the ancient rules of evidence: but in Pennsylvania no similar exigency exists. A disposition has always been evinced by the judiciary to accommodate the law to new requisitions. In this spirit the circle of objections to the *competency* of wit-

* Dato jurejurando, non aliud quæritur, quam an juratum sit: remissa quæstione an debeatur: quasi satis probatum sit jurejurando. ff. L. xii. tit. ii. I. 5. § 2.

nesses has been narrowed, with a proportionable extension of those to the *credibility*. In the case of Garwood-*v*-Dennis,* Chief Justice Tilghman said that necessity, either absolute or moral, would be sufficient ground for dispensing with the usual rules of evidence: and it had before been decided that the strictness of the latter was not applicable to the affairs of merchants.† If any of the rules of evidence are found to possess inconveniences irremediable by the judiciary, the defect may be supplied by the legislature, without having recourse to the bill of discovery.

It results from the preceding observations, that as the principles of equity are already incorporated in *our* common law, the only impediments to its full administration arise from a deficiency of adequate forms to bring the objects of chancery jurisdiction within the power of a court and jury.

The judges of ancient times, from an overstrained timidity, affected to consider the whole field of law included in the writs in the register, and refused to administer justice, except in the forms there prescribed.‡ The new requisitions of the times were unheeded, and

* 4 Bin. Rep. 327.

† Riche et al.-*v*-Broadfield, 1 Dall. 17. This case was decided in 1768.—S. P. Arnold-*v*-Anderson, 2 Yeates, 93.—So in Hill-*v*-Ely, 5 Serg. & R. 365, the *parol* evidence upon which a court of chancery will raise an equity *dehors* a written instrument, was held admissible in our courts of law. See Thomson-*v*-White, 1 Dall. 427.

‡ The original writ of assize of nuisance was directed only against the person who levied the nuisance; so that if the estate were aliened, the injured party remained, according to

while every thing else was in a state of progression, the law remained stationary and without improvement. To remedy this improper deficiency, it was provided by the statute of Westminster the second, that whenever it should occur that a remedy was offered for a particular injury, while none was afforded in another case falling within a like right,* and requiring similar redress, the clerks of chancery should agree upon a new writ, or adjourn the complainants to the next parliament; and a writ should there be framed by the consent of the skilled in the law, lest the courts of the king should be deficient in doing justice.† But though this statute received the highest praise of the ancient lawyers, it does not appear that its beneficial results were equal to the expectations that might reasonably have been entertained. The writs devised in the body of the act were adopted in practice, and a few others framed according to its provisions:‡ but the jealousy of the chancellors, who were already grasping at judicial powers, effectually defeated the wise intentions of the legislature.

It is the opinion of Blackstone,§ that with accuracy in the clerks of chancery, and liberality in the judges, in extending rather than narrowing the operation of writs, this provision would have answered all the purposes of a court of equity, except a discovery by the

this judicial construction, without remedy. This was the efficient cause of the enacting of the statute of Westminster the second. 3 Bl. Com. 221.

* In consimili casu.

† 2 Inst. 405. Statute of Westminster the second, cap. 24.

‡ 2 Inst. 407. Only two writs are there cited.

§ 3 Bl. Com. 52.

defendant's oath. If the ancient lawyers, proceeding without a model for imitation, might have liberalised the science so as to exclude a new jurisdiction, how comparatively easy is our task, guided as we are by the progress of liberal jurisprudence, and the experience of the failure of our ancestors.*

Next to the framing of new writs to include cases yet unprovided for, most important advantages might be derived from the simplification of neglected actions, and an extension of their remedial effects. It seems to have been acknowledged even by the ancient lawyers, that the essoins, vouchers, protections, and imparlances admitted in their practice, tended only to delay the proceedings, without any commensurate benefit. The assize of *novel disseisin*, is said by Sir Edward Coke to be not only *maximè festinum, sed maximè beneficiale*, on account of its freedom from these useless trammels.† There are yet subsisting in ancient actions, other similar impediments, which, it is believed, might without danger be removed.

The great outlines of jurisprudence, the boundaries of right and wrong, are the peculiar objects of legislative cognisance, and should never be extended or restricted by a less powerful authority. But the mere formal parts of justice, such as the framing of a writ and

* In Ohio (3 Griffith's Law Register, 389,) and Virginia, (Tucker's Note, 3 Bl. Com. 52.) provisions have been made for the framing of new writs, whenever they become necessary.

† 2 Inst. 410. So the statute of Westminster the second, cap. xxv. "Quia non est aliquod breve in cancellaria, per quod querentes habent tam festinum remedium sicut per breve novæ disseisinæ," &c. 2 Inst. 409.

the conduct of an action, may with safety be confided to our honourable judiciary, without fear of abuse, or possibility of dangerous innovation. It is therefore with great diffidence suggested, that the less profitable labour of similar details might with propriety be conferred upon our Supreme Court, and would be there exercised with the greater advantages derived from long experience and a perfect knowledge of the subject.

If the parliament of England, instead of giving to the chancellor the power of devising new writs as unforeseen cases arose, had conferred it upon the courts of common law, it is probable that both countries would now enjoy a homogeneous system of jurisprudence. Circumstances unforeseen or not understood, rendered the selected channel of all others the least fit for the purpose; and a beneficial provision thus became nugatory and unavailing. Encumbered by these difficulties, and deprived of a source of improvement by its ambitious rival, it was solely owing to the constancy and firmness of its judges, that the glorious system of the common law survived the united efforts of the numerous tribunals that struggled during so many centuries to make the civil law the law of the English kingdom.

It is time to conclude an essay which has already been extended to a length far exceeding the original intentions of the writer. The jurisprudence of Pennsylvania is a field at once so vast and so new, that it is difficult to examine any of its important branches, without exceeding ordinary limits. When this circumstance is connected with the inexperience of a student, it is hoped that it will afford an apology for his trespasses.

APPENDIX.

A brief sketch of the various forms under which the powers of chancery have been introduced into the other states of the confederation, will, perhaps, not prove uninteresting to those who are desirous of tracing the progress and improvements of American jurisprudence. For the various regulations upon this subject, obligation is, in general, due to Mr. Griffith's Law Register: but in some instances, on account of alterations in laws, recourse has been had to the original sources of information. A few facts have been added, derived from the histories of the states.

I. Those states in which the administration of equity is perfectly distinct from that of law.

In *Delaware* the powers and principles of equity are upon the same footing as in England. The court of chancery is distinct from the courts of law, exercises an exclusive jurisdiction, and has the custody of ideots, lunatics, &c. The proceedings are the same as those of the English court; and the appeal is to the court of errors.

In *New Jersey*, the governor, since the year 1705, has always presided ex-officio, over the court of chancery. The ordinary or legal, and the extraordinary or equitable jurisdictions of the English chancellor are imitated as closely as the diversity of governments would permit. The cause is commenced by bill and subpœna; but in some other respects, the proceedings have been altered by the legislature in order to render them less tedious and expensive.

The general powers of chancery were exercised by the governor of *South Carolina* before the revolution. The state is now divided into four equity circuits. The circuits are sub-divided into twenty districts, in each of which a circuit court of chancery is held by one of *five* chancellors. They exercise their powers, almost in the same manner as in England, and according to the same principles. An appeal lies to the court of appeals in equity, over which the five preside.

The state of *Mississippi* is divided into an eastern and a western district, in each of which a court of chancery is held by the chancellor of the state. The powers and proceedings of this court are as strictly upon the English model as the nature of a republican government will admit. The appeal is to the supreme court of the state.

II. Those states in which equity is only partially committed to distinct courts.

In the state of *New York*, the establishment of a court of

chancery, in which the governor and his council sat, was almost coeval with the English conquest. It is probable that this was the model imitated by Sir William Keith; and as the same objectionable causes existed, the court, like its sister in Pennsylvania, became obnoxious to the people. On the 6th November, 1735, (about two months before the same step was taken in this province,) a spirited, but unsuccessful remonstrance was presented by the legislature, declaring the court to be contrary to law, unwarrantable, and of dangerous consequences to the liberty of the people. Under the present constitution equity is brought home to the door of every citizen. The state is divided into a number of circuits, in each of which a circuit judge presides, who in addition to a general *legal* jurisdiction, enjoys limited chancery powers, with an appeal to the chancellor. This last officer, besides the appellate cognisance, enjoys an original equitable authority, almost co-extensive with that of the English chancellor, and administered through the medium of the same forms.

In *Maryland* the county courts are courts of law and equity; but the two branches are administered separately and on different sides. In all cases within their jurisdiction they are invested with full chancery powers, and concurrently with the chancellor, they have cognisance of pleas relating to ideots and lunatics. The court of chancery, whose jurisdiction over the whole state is solely equitable, in addition to a concurrence in all points with the county courts, has the superintendance of the interests of minors, though not the guardianship of their persons. In both of these courts the practice is modelled upon that of England; appeals from their decisions lie to the court of appeals.

In *Virginia*, as in Maryland, the county courts have both legal and equitable powers; the latter, with a few trifling exceptions, to as great an extent as the English chancellor. They have the custody of the estates and persons of ideots, lunatics, and infants, and may delegate their powers to committees and guardians. The state is divided into nine districts, in each of which a superior court of chancery is held by one of the four chancellors. Besides an appellate jurisdiction from the county courts, they have original cognisance of all causes in chancery, in which the matter in dispute is of the value of thirty-three dollars and thirty-three cents, or more. Their powers and practice are the same as those of the English court, except that they are courts of record, and may enforce their decrees by common law executions, as well as by sequestration and attachment. Appeals may be made to the court of appeals.

The circuit courts of *Missouri* exercise their mixed jurisdiction of law and equity, on different sides of the court, and the appeal from their decrees, in cases of the latter nature, is to the chancellor of the state. The superior court of chancery, in which he presides, has the same powers, and proceeds in the same manner as that of England, with the addition of the enforcement of its decrees at pleasure, by common law executions.

III. Those states in which jurisdiction of the common law and the general powers of equity are vested in one tribunal.

The supreme court of the state of *Vermont* exercises both legal and equitable powers—has the custody of infants, ideots, and lunatics; and proceeds by bill and subpœna. Decrees are enforced by chancery and common law executions, indiscriminately.

In *Connecticut*, the county courts, superior court, and supreme court of errors, are courts both of law and equity. The first holds cognisance when the sum in dispute does not exceed three hundred and thirty-three dollars: the second in all other cases; and the last, as its name imports, has only appellate jurisdiction. Their proceedings are by bill and subpœna, as in England.

In *North Carolina* the county courts are invested with the chancery power to appoint guardians to minors, and with the cognisance of all matters relating to their persons and estates. From their decrees the appeal is to the superior court of law and equity, which, with the single exception just mentioned, has exclusive original jurisdiction of all matters in equity. The commencement of the term is usually devoted to the ordinary legal business, and on the last days the judges sit as chancellors. The proceedings are by bill and subpœna, as in England, and the appeal to the supreme court of the state.

The only courts which possess chancery powers in *Georgia*, are the superior courts held in each county of the state. The mode of exercising their powers varies very materially from the English practice. The bill is sanctioned by the judge, at his chambers, and the usual chancery proceedings are had until the cause is ready for trial, which is by special jury. If parties conceive that the verdict was given against evidence, or that the law was mistaken by the judge, their only redress is by an application for a new trial, as this is the highest judicial tribunal in the state. The decree is enforced in the same manner as a judgment at law.

In *Ohio*, the supreme court and the several courts of common pleas are courts of law and equity, possessing and exercising all the functions of the latter, proceeding by bill and subpœna, as in England, and enforcing their decrees as well by chancery process as by common law executions.

In the circuit courts of the several counties of *Indiana*, causes at common law and equity are tried promiscuously, according to the direction of the court, and convenience of the parties. The proceedings are according to the English practice, with the exception that where the judgment is for money, a common law execution issues.

The circuit courts of *Illinois* have both legal and equitable powers. The proceedings are by bill and subpœna, and the decree is enforced by common law executions. An appeal lies to the supreme court of the state.

In *Kentucky* the circuit and general courts are courts both of law and equity, each of which branches is administered on a separate side. The proceedings in general conform with those of England, with the additional power of issuing common law executions.

In *Tennessee* the chancery powers of the county courts extend only to the custody of infants, ideots, and lunatics. The circuit courts have general and original jurisdiction of all cases in equity, and are governed in their proceedings and decrees, with a few exceptions, by the English rules and practice. Matters of fact are tried by a jury, and a new trial may be granted as at law. Decrees are enforced by common law executions as well as by the processes of sequestration and attachment. The supreme court of errors and appeals has an appellate jurisdiction from the circuit courts, and also a concurrent original cognisance of matters in equity.

In *Alabama* the circuit courts have original chancery jurisdiction, and proceed by bill and subpœna. The appeal is to the supreme court of the state. Executions may issue against the body, goods, or lands of the defendant, and where specific performance of a contract for the sale of land is sought, the court may decree a title.

IV. Those states in which there are no courts exercising general chancery powers.

In *Maine* the chancery powers of the supreme judicial court extend only to the authorising of executors and administrators to sell real estate, in order to pay debts, legacies, and taxes, when the personalty is insufficient; and the guardians of minors and non compotes to make a provision for their maintenance and support, and for their personal interest.

In *New Hampshire* the only chancery power known to the law is the superintendance exercised by the superior court over property appointed to charitable uses.

In *Rhode Island* the powers of chancery exercised by the supreme judicial court are restricted to the single case of mortgages.

A court of chancery never existed in *Massachusetts*. At the present day the supreme court and the several courts of common pleas are courts of law, possessing limited equity powers. When judgment has been obtained for the penalty or forfeiture of a bond or mortgage, they may make up their decrees so as to hinder the plaintiff from recovering more than he ought in equity. Mortgagors, or other persons claiming under them, may have their bills in equity to redeem. A late act (1818) has vested in the supreme court exclusively, the power to hear and determine all cases of trust, arising under deeds, wills, or in the settlement of estates, and contracts in writing, of which a party claims a specific performance, and in which there is not a plain, adequate, and complete remedy at law. In these cases there are two modes of proceeding: the first is by inserting the bill in the attachment or summons; and the second is the ordinary chancery mode, by subpœna. They may also authorise executors, administrators, and guardians, to sell real estate for the payment of debts and legacies. The supreme judicial court may issue all such processes as may be necessary in order to carry into effect the powers granted to it: but decrees for money are usually executed like judgments at common law.

In *Louisiana* there is no distinction between equity and law, or between the legal and equitable powers of courts of justice. As their law assumes to be founded on the principles of natural reason, and not on artificial rules, it does not require to be modified in particular cases by a court of special jurisdiction. The principles of the English courts of equity, which are in general derived from the civil law, are a part of their system of jurisprudence, which also traces its origin to that source. Their proceedings in civil cases are by petition and answer, without any particular forms of action. The petition states the case, and may or may not require the defendant to set forth his answer upon oath to particular facts. The trial is by jury if either party require it.

CONTENTS.

CONTENTS.

ERRATA.

Note † p. 10. For *preætriit* read *præteriit.*
Note * p. 15. For *prætuxtu* read *prætextu.*
Note * p. 16. After *affingere* add *debent.*
Same note for *sar* read *sur.* For *sot* read *sont.*
Page 32. For *county* read *country.*
Page. 53. For *stature* read *statute.*
Note ‡ p. 54. Add Jones-*v*-Peterman, 3 Serg. and R. 547, and Thomson-*v*-White 1 Dall. 427.
Page 116. For *forcement* read *deforcement.*

REPRINTS OF LEGAL CLASSICS PUBLISHED BY THE LAWBOOK EXCHANGE, LTD.

TREATISES

Beth, Loren P. *The American Theory of Church and State.* Gainesville: University of Florida Press, 1958. vii, 183 pp. Reprinted 2002 by The Lawbook Exchange, Ltd. LCCN 2001023455. ISBN 1-58477-179-8. Cloth. $65.
* Beth questions the relevance of the principle of the separation of church and state in light of the modern American political system and modern society in general. In his impassioned theory, Beth advocates in favor of the concept, and supports this thesis with a historical perspective that traces the idea from its origins in seventeenth-century English thought to the present day.

Black, Henry Campbell. *A Treatise on the Law of Income Taxation under Federal and State Laws.* Kansas City: Vernon Law Book Co., 1913. xlii, 403 pp. Reprint available 2002 by The Lawbook Exchange, Ltd. ISBN 1-58477-237-9. Cloth. $85.
* In 1913 the Sixteenth Amendment, which authorized income taxation, was ratified by the required three-fourths majority of states. Black [1860-1927] published this work soon after this historic event in order to define the nature of taxable income, explain the history of income taxation, and defend the government's right to impose it. He is guided throughout by a Progressive-Era belief in the federal government as an agent of social reform. Black is also the author of the well-known *Law Dictionary.*

Brackenridge, Hugh. *Law Miscellanies: Containing an Introduction to the Study of Law; notes on Blackstone's Commentaries, Shewing the Variations of the Law of Pennsylvania from the Law of England, and what Acts of Assembly Might Require to be Repealed or Modified Observations on Smith's Edition of the Laws of Pennsylvania; Strictures on Decisions of the Supreme Court of the United States, and on Certain Acts of Congress, with Some Law Cases, and a Variety of Other Matters, Chiefly Original.* Philadelphia: P. Byrne, 1814. 588 pp. Reprinted 2001 by The Lawbook Exchange, Ltd. LCCN 00-059548. ISBN 1-58477-161-5. Cloth. $100.
* Facsimile reprint of the 1814 original edition. Described by Charles Warren as one of the four early American general works on the Common Law that "showed genuine scientific thought and research and have remained of more or less permanent value in American legal literature." *A History of the American Bar* 335-336. Brackenridge [1748-1816], published this, his most important legal work while he was a Supreme

Court Justice of Pennsylvania. *Dictionary of American Biography* I:544-545. Eller, *The William Blackstone Collection in the Yale Law Library* 142 and Cohen, *Bibliography of Early American Law* 5375.

Elias, Gbolahan. *Explaining Constructive Trusts.* Oxford: Clarendon Press; Oxford University Press, 1990. xxii, 177 pp. Reprinted 2002 by The Lawbook Exchange, Ltd. ISBN 1-58477-208-5. Cloth. $75.

* Concerned with "rationalizing the rules" (Preface p. v) of constructive trusts, this reappraisal of the English law of trusts discounts two major existing theses regarding the rules (first, that, based on the North American experience, they should be considered as instruments of restitution; and second, that they are disorganized) and advances Elias' new thesis that "the rules should be regarded as instruments for the rational furtherance of three good aims: (1) making disponors abide by their dispositions...(2) making those who gain through loss to others give the gains up to those others...(3) making those who inflict losses on others repair those losses..." (Preface p. v). Revision of the author's Ph.D. thesis at Oxford University. Prof. Lionel Smith, a distinguished international expert in the law of trusts, notes about this work: "Elias' book Explaining Constructive Trusts, marks an important landmark in the development of this legal institution. Elias explained and ultimately rejected two extreme ways of understanding the constructive trust. On the one hand is the thesis, still widely accepted in North America, that all constructive trusts arise to prevent unjust enrichment. On the other hand is the traditional view, still popular in England, that constructive trusts respond to such a wide range of situations that it is impossible to classify them in any meaningful way in terms of their causative events. Elias developed an intermediate thesis in which the known constructive trusts could be grouped into coherent but differentiated categories. Some do indeed arise to prevent unjust enrichment; but others arise to perfect a party's intention in relation to the disposition of his assets; and still other cases in which the language of constructive trust have been used are actually cases of compensation for loss wrongfully caused. Much of the subsequent work on understanding constructive trusts has been built on these foundations."

Freeman, A.C. *A Treatise of the Law of Judgments. Including All Final Determinations of the Rights of Parties in Actions or Proceedings at Law or in Equity. Revised, and Greatly Enlarged by Edward W. Tuttle.* San Francisco: Bancroft-Whitney, 1925. Three volumes. 1216; 1280; 1264 pp. Reprinted 1993 by The Lawbook Exchange, Ltd. LCCN 99-047228. ISBN 0-9630106-6-2. Cloth. $295.

* Considered by Vanderbilt to be one of the great textbooks in which the history of American law might well be traced. *Men and Measures in the Law*, p. 21. In the present treatise (which cites over 35,000 cases), the editor has analyzed the cases with care.... The book will be of great assistance to lawyers searching for authorities in the important field it covers. *Harvard Law Review* 32(2):283-5.

Gilmore, Grant. *Security Interests in Personal Property.* Boston: Little, Brown & Company, 1965. Two volumes. xxxiv, 651; xiii, 653-1508 pp. Reprinted 1999 by The Lawbook Exchange, Ltd. LCCN 99-10258. ISBN 1-886363-81-1. Cloth. $195.
* Written by the late Grant Gilmore, Co-Reporter for Article 9 of the Uniform Commercial Code, this landmark work, often cited, is extremely well respected as an acknowledged authority in this area. Combines an engrossing account of the drafting of Article 9 as it emerged in its final form with important interpretive data relating to security interests. This title is the recipient of both the Order of the Coif and the James Barr Ames award. Now back in print and of continued relevance today.

Gould, James. *A Treatise on the Principles of Pleading in Civil Action.* Boston: Lilly and Wait, 1832. x, 536 pp. Reprinted 2002 by The Lawbook Exchange, Ltd. LCCN 00-059549. ISBN 1-58477-158-5. Cloth. $95.
* Gould [1770-1838] was the preeminent law professor at Litchfield Law School, the nation's first law school. This treatise is taken from his Litchfield lectures and puts forth his system of principles of pleading in an orderly and scientific, reasonable manner. "Gould's Pleading is a legal classic of the highest order, and has placed its author among the very best legal writers of the age." Marvin, *Legal Bibliography* 342. *Dictionary of American Biography* IV:453-454. *Catalogue of the Library of the Law School of Harvard University* (1909) I:775.

Greenleaf, Simon. *A Treatise on the Law of Evidence.* Boston: Little, Brown, and Company, 1899. Three volumes. Reprinted 2001 by The Lawbook Exchange, Ltd. LCCN 00-065554. ISBN 1-58477-116-X. Cloth. $350.
* Sixteenth edition and last edition. The first volume of this edition was edited by John H. Wigmore just prior to the publication of his magnum opus on this subject. Thus this edition represents the transition from *Greenleaf on Evidence* to *Wigmore on Evidence.* The second and third volumes were edited by E.A. Harriman. According to Marvin, "Until the appearance of Professor Greenleaf's *Treatise upon Evidence*, the Bar in the United States were wholly dependent upon English works for information in this department of the law." Marvin 347-348, citing earlier eds.

Hurst, James Willard. *Law and Markets in United States History: Different Modes of Bargaining among Interests.* [Madison]: The University of Wisconsin Press, [1982]. vii, 207 pp. Reprinted 2001 by The Lawbook Exchange, Ltd. LCCN 00-067116. ISBN 1-58477-136-4. Cloth. $80.
* The eminent legal scholar's sociological analysis of the relation between law and private business (using the lumber business as an example) in relation to society at large. He argues that law and business support the same goals of efficiency and humanity, and examines their interrelationship toward that end in terms of ethical issues related to public policy, money supply, the impact of incremental change,

inflation and deflation, monopoly and competition, and other economic factors. Based on Hurst's lectures at The University of Wisconsin in April, 1981.

Laussat, Antony. *An Essay on Equity in Pennsylvania.* Philadelphia: Published for the Institution, by Robert Desilver, 1826. vi, [7]-157, [2] pp. Reprint available 2002 by The Lawbook Exchange, Ltd. LCCN 00-067115. ISBN 1-58477-139-9. Cloth. $60.
* Written in 1825 and submitted as a dissertation to the Law Academy of Philadelphia. Laussat [1806-1833], a Philadelphia lawyer, traces the history of equity in the state, paying particular attention to the influence of Quaker beliefs and English Common Law. Although the work takes as its subject the law of equity in Pennsylvania, he views equity in its most profound sense, as the foundation of moral law. This study received high praise from Chancellor Kent, John Marshall, and George Sharswood. Cohen, *Bibliography of Early American Law* 4976.

Lieber, Francis. *On Civil Liberty and Self-government. Enlarged edition in one volume.* Philadelphia: J.B. Lippincott & Co.. 1859. xix, [15]-629 pp. Reprinted 2001 by The Lawbook Exchange, Ltd. LCCN 99-056928. ISBN 1-58477-070-8. Cloth. $100.
* "In these volumes Lieber presented the first systematic works on political science that appeared in America... he retains credit as a notable pioneer with wide influence in more than one generation." DAB VI:236-238. Widely read and used as a textbook, this is the best known of Lieber's work. Lieber [1800-1872], a German scholar and political activist who suffered persecution from the Prussians, was early associated with the historian Niebuhr. He immigrated to the United States in 1827, and his writings, among them an encyclopedia that was the foundation of the *Encyclopedia Britannica*, advanced his reputation. He became professor of history and political economy at South Carolina College, and was later appointed to the same chair in Columbia College. In 1865 he moved to Columbia Law School, where he was known to be a prominent political philosopher and consultant to the Union government, due to his influential writings on military law. Enlarged edition in one volume, having first been published in two volumes in 1853. Cohen, *Bibliography of Early American Law* 3369. Sabin, *A Dictionary of Books Relating to America* 40974. *Catalogue of the Library of the Law School of Harvard University* (1909) I:1176. *Dictionary of American Biography* VI:236-238.

Pothier,R.J. *Treatise on the Contract of Sale.* Translated from the French by L.S. Cushing. Boston: Charles C. Little and James Brown, 1839. xvi, 406 pp. Reprinted 2000 by The Lawbook Exçhange, Ltd. LCCN 99-10260. ISBN 1-886363-82-X. Cloth. $70.
* By the well-known French jurist Pothier [1699-1772], who followed his *A Treatise of Obligations* with a series of treatises on branches of the law based on Roman and French law. This particular treatise, on the importance of sale as a contract, is a reprint of the first American edition which was translated by Luther Stearns Cushing [1803-1856], who lectured on Roman law at Harvard.

Pothier, Robert Joseph. *A Treatise on the Law of Obligations, or Contracts. Translated from the French, with an Introduction, Appendix, and Notes, Illustrative of the English Law on the Subject. By William David Evans.* London: A. Strahan, 1802. Two volumes. [1], 578, [1]; iv, 715, [1]pp. Reprinted 2000 by The Lawbook Exchange, Ltd. LCCN 99-26397. ISBN 1-886363-98-6. Cloth. $195.

* Of this edition Marvin speaks highly of Evans: "His notes are comprehensive and learned, and deserve a careful perusal in connexion with the text, and he is entitled to considerable praise for having furnished *Pothier on Obligations* to the profession in so good and accurate an English garb." Marvin, *Legal Bibliography* 578. Holdsworth agrees: "He helped to make English lawyers acquainted with Pothier's work, and, by so doing, did considerable service to the development of the English law of contract..." Holdsworth, *A History of English Law* XIII:467. Evans [1767-1821] was a scholarly English lawyer. To Pothier's work he added an Appendix on several topics of English law, organized as a treatise on the law of evidence. Pothier's treatise on civil law was "... soon recognized as a major contribution to legal science, translated by Evans and frequently cited in British Courts." Walker, *Oxford Companion to Law* 973. Reprint of the uncommon Evans translation, the English second edition which followed the American edition of 1802 (translated by F.X. Martin), which is also available as a facsimile reprint published by The Lawbook Exchange, Ltd.

Pothier, Robert Joseph. *A Treatise on Obligations, Considered in a Moral and Legal View. Translated from the French of Pothier. Translated by Francois-Xavier Martin.* Newburn, N.C.: Martin & Ogden, 1802. 2 vols. in 1 book. Reprinted 2000 by The Lawbook Exchange, Ltd. With a new introduction by Warren M. Billings. LCCN 98-38360. ISBN 1-886363-62-5. Cloth. $75.

* Pothier was a jurist and legal scholar who specialized in French and Roman law. In the decades that led up to the Civil War, this classic, highly-regarded civil law treatise was required reading for practitioners, scholars, as well as law students. Martin, a printer from New Bern, North Carolina, gained distinction for this translation, which he published in 1802.

"The *Treatise on Obligations* was soon recognized as a major contribution to legal science, translated by Evans and frequently cited in British Courts." Walker 973. Marvin quotes Sir William Jones' introduction of Pothier's *Obligations* to the bar in England: "For my own part, I am so charmed with them, that if my undissembled fondness for the study of jurisprudence, were never to produce any greater benefit to the public, than barely the introduction of Pothier to the acquaintances of my countrymen, I should think that I had, in some measure, discharged the debt which every man, according to Lord Coke owes to his profession." Marvin, *Legal Bibliography* 578. Cohen, *Bibliography of Early American Law* 3656.

Rogers, Edward S. *Good Will Trade-Marks and Unfair Trading.* Chicago: A.W. Shaw Company, [1914]. 288 pp. Reprint available 2002 by The Lawbook Exchange, Ltd. LCCN 2001045971. ISBN 1-58477-211-5. Cloth. $70.

* Rogers [b. 1875] was a lecturer on the law of trademarks at the University of Michigan Law School. This volume examines such topics as fair use, the extent of trademark coverage, and types of infringement. Also considers issues related to dishonest advertisements and other printed materials.

Sears, John H. *Trust Estates as Business Companies.* [*Second Edition*]. Kansas City, Mo.: Vernon Law Book Company, 1921. xx, 782 pp. [1921]. Reprinted 1998 by The Lawbook Exchange, Ltd. LCCN 97-32423 ISBN 1-886363-41-2. Cloth. $95.

* Sears invented the term "trust estates as business companies" which was recognized and defined in *Rawle's Third Revision of Bouvier's Law Dictionary.* A practical description of the law of trusts including historical perspectives into the origin of the modern "Massachusetts Business trust," arguably the only common-law method of business organization available with limited liability for the organizers, including the *Standard Oil Trust.* The text also includes a discussion of income taxation which is still of continued relevance in today's tax law, discussions of "Common Law Companies," "Business Trusts" and "Voluntary Associations" and relevant Massachusetts and Oklahoma statutes. The second edition is a significant update to the original 1912 edition.

Story, Joseph. *Commentaries on the Conflict of Laws, Foreign and Domestic, in Regard to Contracts, Rights, and Remedies, and Especially in Regard to Marriages, Divorces, Wills, Successions, and Judgments. Second Edition. Revised, Corrected and Greatly Enlarged.* London: A. Maxwell, 1841. xxxiv, 927 pp. (misnumbered in original, PP. 753-756 omitted.) Reprinted 2001 by The Lawbook Exchange, Ltd. ISBN 1-58477-145-3. Cloth. $125.

* With William Kent, Joseph Story shares the distinction of having had the greatest influence on American law during the nineteenth century. Marvin considers Story's Conflict of Laws to be the first systematic work on the subject. Story collected material from all available sources, and systematized it in a manner useful to all practitioners. "No work on international jurisprudence merited, nor received, greater praise from the jurists of Europe. It impressed English lawyers with the highest respect for the extensive learning of Mr. Justice Story." Marvin, *Legal Bibliography* (1847) 670-671. "It is not too much to say that its publication constituted an epoch in the law; for it became at once the standard and almost the sole authority...[it] received the honor of being practically the first American law book to be cited as authority in English courts." Marke, *A Catalogue of the Law Collection at New York University* (1953) 358. This facsimile reprint of the second edition published in London is the final authorial edition, produced "under the direction and sanction of the learned author." Sweet and Maxwell, *A Legal Bibliography of the British Commonwealth of Nations* XV:337. *Catalogue*

of the Library of the Law School of Harvard University (1909) II:669, citing 2nd Boston ed. Parrish, 'Law Books and Legal Publishing in America, 1760-1840,' in *Law Library J.* (72:355-452) 434, citing 2nd Boston ed. Cohen, *Bibliography of Early American Law* 2725, citing 2nd Boston ed.

Tiedeman, Christopher G. *A Treatise on State and Federal Control of Persons and Property in the United States Considered from both a Civil and Criminal Standpoint.* St. Louis: The F.H. Thomas Law Book Co., 1900. Two volumes. Reprint available 2002 by The Lawbook Exchange, Ltd. ISBN 1-58477-229-8. Cloth. $195.

* A conservative jurist known for his important study A Treatise on the Limitations of Police Power in the United States Considered from Both a Civil and Criminal Standpoint, Tiedeman [1857-1903] completed this work at a time when the spirit of social and economic laissez-faire of the Gilded Age was giving way to demands for greater degrees of governmental regulation in response to the emergence of modern corporate capitalism and, especially, the rapid growth of Socialism, Communism, and Anarchism. For Tiedeman, the fundamental issue is the need to control these groups in the interests of public order while preserving their rights of self-determination as guaranteed by the Constitution. He is optimistic that popular faith in the Constitution is strong enough to maintain this delicate balance.

Wheaton, Henry. *Elements of International Law: with a Sketch of the History of the Science.* Philadelphia: Carey, Lea & Blanchard, 1836. xiv, 375 pp. Reprinted 2002 by The Lawbook Exchange, Ltd. LCCN 00-066335. ISBN 1-58477-170-4. Cloth. $80.

* Reprint of the first edition of this important treatise on international law by the distinguished lawyer and diplomat. The work enjoyed numerous later editions and translations. "Mr. Wheaton's early familiarity with the jurisprudence and foreign relations of the United States, his long experience in diplomacy, his intimate acquaintance with European languages and foreign diplomatic writers, entitles his writings upon International Law to more than ordinary consideration. His works enjoy the highest reputation for the soundness of their views, and the learning and research displayed in illustrating the various topics discussed." Marvin, *Legal Bibliography* (1847) 728, citing third edition. "On his own merits Wheaton is clearly entitled to rank among the classics. Like Grotius, he embodied a happy combination of profound scholarship with a wide experience of diplomatic and public life, and his work further resembles that of Grotius in that it cannot be classified under the conventional labels of any doctrinal system. His insistence upon the fundamental principles of natural law is balanced by his analysis of practice as an immediate source of positive law." H.A. Smith, *Law Quarterly Review* 307-308. Marke, *A Catalogue of the Law Collection at New York University* (1953) 584, citing 8th ed. Sabin, *A Dictionary of Books Relating to America* 103156. Cohen, *Bibliography of Early American Law* 7200. Sweet and Maxwell, *A Legal Bibliography of the British Commonwealth of Nations* II:377. *Catalogue of the Library of the Law School of Harvard University* (1909) II:905.

Wiener, Frederick Bernays. *Briefing and Arguing Federal Appeals.* xvi, 506 pp. Washington, D.C.: BNA Incorporated, 1961. xvi, 506 pp. Reprinted with a new introduction by Bryan A. Garner. Reprinted 2001 by The Lawbook Exchange, Ltd. LCCN 2001031682. ISBN 1-58477-183-6. Cloth. $85.

* In addition to his discussion of the importance of appellate advocacy and a description of the manner in which federal appellate courts (Supreme Court, U.S. Court of Appeals, and specialized federal courts) deal with appeals, this important volume provides guidelines and suggestions for the finer points of writing briefs and appeals and oral arguments. With a new introduction by Bryan A. Garner, editor of *Black's Law Dictionary, 7th edition.*

Wrightington, Sydney R. *The Law of Unincorporated Associations and Similar Relations.* Boston: Little, Brown, and Company, 1916. xxvi, 486 pp. Reprint available 2002 by The Lawbook Exchange, Ltd. LCCN 2001045970. ISBN 1-58477-205-0. Cloth. $125.

* "The first edition of this book was a pioneer work, and a distinct service to practitioners. It sought, within the compass of a moderate-sized volume, to treat comprehensively the law relating to all kinds of associations, whether or not organized for profit, not including corporations." Marke, *A Catalogue of the Law Collection at New York University* 746. With an appendix of forms.